From Millstone To Milestone

How To Get Out Of Debt Using 3 Simple Steps.

Bob Marette

Foreword By John Cummuta

Author Of The Transforming Debt Into Wealth® System And Are You Being Seduced Into Debt?

16
EasyRead Large

RHYW

Copyright Page from the Original Book

Bridge-Logos
Alachua, Florida 32615 USA

From Millstone to Milestone
By Bob Marette

www.bobmarette.com

Revised Edition, 2008
Second Printing, 2011
Bridge Logos edition 2013

Published by: IMD Press

Library of Congress Catalog Card Number: 2013942442
International Standard Book Number: 978-1-61036-114-9

Printed in United States of America

TABLE OF CONTENTS

Get Out of Debt in Five to Seven Years, Including Mortgage by Applying God's Principles

Revised Edition

Here is what stewardship experts are saying about this book:

Bob has given us tremendous wisdom and counsel by writing a book that is timeless. His advice is as relevant today as it was twenty and thirty years ago and will continue to be relevant twenty to thirty years from now. This book should be read by everyone. To those who are in debt there are practical steps for getting out of debt, and to those who have no debt, this book will affirm and encourage them. I endorse it wholeheartedly.

Ron Blue, President
Kingdom Advisors

Bob Marette has a passion for getting God's people out of debt so they can be free to serve Christ. In this book, Bob talks about the two "critical, foundational principles" that *every* Christian needs to know *before* embarking on their debt elimination program. This book is so practical, which makes getting out of debt—no matter how deep the hole—a very real possibility.

Howard Dayton
Co-founder with Larry Burkett, Crown Financial Ministries

Bob's heart and the excellent counsel and clear steps he outlines make this a valuable book for anyone wishing to get out of debt as quickly as possible. The time frame required will depend on the situation and more importantly, commitment—but Bob provides the "how to." As we say in *Good $ense,* "You can do it!"

Dick Towner
Executive Director, Good $ense Movement with the Willow
Creek Association

This is a *two thumbs up* book in a world where many people's finances are experiencing *two thumbs down.*

Brian Kluth

Author of the best-selling *40-Day Spiritual Journey to a More Generous Life* devotional

If you want to get out of debt quickly—including your mortgage—and build wealth safely, there is no better method than the one in this book. I know, because I have personally followed Bob's strategies with tremendous financial success. This book is biblical, easy to understand, and financially sound. It will change your life. I'll be buying it for all of my friends and recommending it to all of my clients.

Rod Rogers
Author, *Pastor Driven Stewardship: 10 Steps to Lead Your Church to Biblical Giving* and *The Dynamic Giving System*

Every once in a while someone comes along who makes the difficult to comprehend rather easy to understand. Bob Marette is that leader. I highly recommend *From Millstone to Milestone* book and workshops to all who want to advance in their ministry and family finances. You couldn't find a more caring and informative leader on Christian financial topics for a seminar in your church.

Scott Preissler, Ph.D.
Department of Stewardship—School of Theology
Southwestern Baptist Theological Seminary

I love books that help raise up stewards to be rich toward God and this is one of them! This book outlines biblical principles which can set people free from service to mammom, and it provides practical ideas for anyone to begin a journey of fruitful service to God.

Gary Hoag
Generosity Monk

A very practical book loaded with ideas and suggestions. You can easily pick and choose—but be sure to understand the 'three-legged stool'! Bob Marette will help you to make solid financial decisions in a debt-ridden society!

Dr Gene Getz
President, Center for Church Renewal

Bob is a man of commitment and integrity. He is passionate about helping the Body of Christ escape the bondage of financial debt. The plan he teaches in the book is incredible. It is one of the best I have seen. In addition to the fact that it works, it is based on the wonderful Word of God. If you will work this plan, it will work for you. You can indeed be set free from debt much faster than you ever thought possible!

Bruce Ammons
Author, *Conquering Debt God's Way*

Totally debt free, including your mortgage? Personal finance expert Bob Marette shows you how! Becoming debt-free is not only doable, but it makes perfect sense, and in this book he coaches you step by step to total financial freedom.

Dan Benson
Author, *12 Stupid Mistakes People Make With Their Money*

Bob clearly demonstrates where debt fits into the Christian World in his new book *From Millstone to Milestone.* He clearly delineates the fact that the Body of Christ has a millstone around its neck, called *debt.* However, he clearly shows us that this does not have to be the way and is not the way that Jesus had in mind for us. If you truly want to know what the Bible has to say about debt, then this is a must read. However, it is more than just a biblical perspective on debt; Bob clearly shows you how to eliminate your debts so that you can truly be in tune with the Lord and clearly see what He has in store for you.

Dave Ireland
President, Invest in Your Debt.com, and author, *Invest in Your Debt*

Over the years that I have personally known Bob, I have not only found him to be a genuine man of God, but also a great teacher. In this book, Bob has taken the practical, down-to-earth, debt-free principles and has brought them to a whole new level of understanding so desperately needed in the Church today, by showing from God's Word why every Christian should be totally debt-free. I know this book will help many families get free from the ravages of debt bondage so that they can fully serve the Lord.

Mel Wild
Debt-Free & Prosperous Living, Inc.

Acknowledgements

God has brought this book about by using many people and circumstances in my life:

My bride of forty years, Deborah Ann, has been my partner through the mountains and valleys of life, and has been used by God as a friend and wise counselor. Her godly intuition has directed me to "lay aside every encumbrance and run the race that is set before me." I look forward to the next forty years, or however long God allows, as we continue to grow closer to each other and to the Lord.

My dad and mom, Harvey and Anna Marette, gave me a foundation for doing the right thing always in my life. This was learned at home and through church in my earlier years.

My father-in-law and my mother-in-law, Blynn and Myrl Stewart, gave me wise counsel on being a husband and a father and taught me what "family" is all about.

My kiddos, Brandon and Brianne, gave Deborah and me much joy over the years. They gave us a sense of pride as we watched them grow to become godly young adults. Now, they are giving us ... grandchildren.

Larry Burkett, the true pioneer of biblical financial teaching, who helped me to see that the Bible truly is the greatest financial book ever written.

My dear friend, Stan Lawson, constantly encouraged me to write and to grow and to do things above what I conceived possible.

My first pastor, Kevin Randolph, challenged me to grow in Christ and become more like Christ in everything I did.

My pastor, my favorite Bible teacher, and my friend, Cary Johnson, encouraged me and taught me to hide God's Word in my heart and to keep in His Word daily.

Pastor Kim Skattum constantly challenges me to take what I have learned over the years as a Christian and to minister to the needs of others.

My Friday morning men's group constantly reminds me to read the Word, meditate on the Word, and obey the Word. Thanks, guys!

The Lord has placed many Bible teachers on the radio to continually challenge and encourage me to live a life of service to others. The list of those godly men is too long for this page, but I feel like I have been individually mentored by the ministries of John MacArthur, Chuck Swindoll, and Charles Stanley.

I want to thank my co-author, the Holy Spirit of God, who brought this book about. It is HIS wisdom on these pages that follow. I simply wrote what HE directed.

Foreword

Two decades ago God tapped me on the shoulder and gave me the assignment to help people get out of debt.

It seemed odd at the time that he would pick me, because I had just clawed my way out of a "buried in debt" situation myself ... but then maybe that's not so odd when you look at some of the characters God used in the Bible.

After guiding me through five years of writing books, recording audios, and doing seminars on personal debt-elimination, the Lord brought Bob Marette into my life ... and then He proceeded to bring Bob into the lives of thousands of others, to help them get out of debt using biblical principles.

Bob became a Certified Seminar Leader and taught in schools and churches in his community. He had a unique and focused zeal to help people, particularly Christians, get out of the world's money system and begin tapping into the power and liberty of God's money system.

It wasn't long before Bob had taken what he had learned, bathed it in Scriptures, and dressed it up in a way that would resonate with Christians and pastors across several states. Today it is obvious that God has continued to bless Bob's ministry, and this book you're now reading is evidence of the Holy Spirit's refinement of the Christian debt-freedom message.

Bob is "the man," in the vernacular, when it comes to teaching the Body of Christ about the godly use of our financial resources ... particularly as it pertains to getting out of debt.

To this day, if anyone asks me about doing debt-freedom seminars in churches, Bob Marette's name is in the first sentence of my answer. I know of no one in the world who does a better job than Bob, and you now hold in your hands the opportunity to tap into his knowledge and wisdom.

Don't pass this opportunity by. The rest of your life will be better for it.

In His Name,
John Cummuta
Author of the *Transforming Debt into Wealth* ® System and *Are You Being Seduced into Debt?*

Introduction

The abuse of credit has become a real problem in the United States, as well as in many other parts of the world. It started small in the 1950s, but has mushroomed into a major part of our lives. The credit industry has become a multi-trillion dollar industry. The United States government has provided us as individuals a terrible example of how to use money.

The problem that has occurred for the Christian is that there is no difference in the use of credit, as compared to the non-Christian. One would think that we, as Christians, would handle our money in a way very different from the world, but that has not happened. As you look at every area of life, there is no distinction from the Christian and the non-Christian. Divorce is rampant on both fronts. Drug use and pornography are major issues for both. Giving to charitable organizations is actually a little higher for the non-Christian than for the Christian giving to the church.

Unfortunately, debt is no different. We, as Christians, have fallen just as hard into the debt trap as non-Christians. We follow the many who "want to get it now." It's called "instant gratification" and it is *so* prevalent. We bury ourselves with monthly payments and then wonder how we got into that hole. The disgusting thing is that for many who call themselves

Christians, bankruptcy is the easy way out. Again, there is no difference in the area of bankruptcy.

Webster defines *millstone* as "a heavy burden." In Matthew 18:6, Jesus says, "but whoever causes one of these little ones who believe in Me to stumble, it would be better for him to have a heavy *millstone* hung around his neck, and to be drowned in the depth of the sea." Picture a person with a large block of concrete around his neck. What would happen if he were thrown into the ocean? There would be very little hope for that person to survive, as he would be carried quickly by that millstone to the bottom of the ocean floor.

The Body of Christ today has a millstone around its neck and that millstone is called "debt." Most people in the Church are buried by debt and feel as if there is very little hope. As a result, they are not able to give to the Lord as they would wish they could. They are not able to serve in the Church as they would like. They are not able to minister to others as they know the Lord has commanded them, because they are so focused on their own situation. They are not able to *go* where the Lord wants to use them.

There are over 2,300 verses in the Bible that relate directly or indirectly to money. That is more than any other subject in the Bible, except "love." Why does God spend so much time talking about money? Is it because money is so important to God? I believe the answer to that question is a resounding "No." I believe that our attitude toward money is what is important to God. Matthew 6:21 states, "For where your treasure is, there will your heart be also." What is important to you (your treasures) will dictate where your heart is.

I think it is time that we, as followers of Jesus Christ, come to realize that God wants for us *His very best* (not the world's best, but *His*). He has given us the guidelines how to achieve the very best *if* only we will follow Him. The problem that arises is threefold: 1) We do not know *what* He says to us about money and debt, because we do not spend time in His Word trying to find out, 2) We have already buried ourselves and do not think there is a way out, and 3) We do not have the discipline or the desire to try to change.

Turn back one page in your dictionary and you will find that Webster defines *milestone* as "a significant point in development." For a person under the weight of the millstone, just easing the weight of that millstone would be a tremendous accomplishment, a "significant point in development." But my goal in this book is not only to help you ease the weight of the millstone, but to give you the tools to totally eliminate it—to move it completely away from your life. This would then be a major accomplishment. Hebrews 12:1 says that we are to "lay aside every encumbrance..., and let us run with endurance the race that is set before us." Getting rid of that encumbrance of debt (the millstone) will enable you to run the race in such a way as to serve the Lord when, where, and how *He* wants (the milestone).

I want to show you how *you* can get out of debt in a short period of time—typically five to seven years, including your mortgage—and how you can be totally *free* from the bondage that you might be in right now. I want to take you *from a millstone* that you are under right now *to a milestone* of being totally out of debt.

I want to encourage you as you read this book to prayerfully ask the Lord this question: "Lord, what can *I* do right now to change this part of my life?" Then ask Him for the strength and desire and will power to make those tough choices. I have to warn you, getting out of debt is only 20 percent knowledge. It is 80 percent behavior, which means we *must* make some changes. These changes will not be major changes, but a series of little changes. I am not going to suggest that you live like a pauper with no fun in your life. That's not what God wants. He said in John 10:10, that He "came that we might have life and might have it abundantly." Be careful, though! This abundant life is not the "abundant life" that the world is trying to sell us. The abundant life that God wants for you and for me is one filled with joy, with integrity, with great relationships with family and friends, and with no financial stress. This life can be yours *if* you follow the principles in this book, because these are the principles in *His* Word.

My prayer for you is that you become debt-free soon so that you can serve the Lord as He wants. However, it's not about something you will achieve five to seven years down the road. It's all about you becoming *today* what He wants you to become. Then you can begin the process of "Getting Out of Debt By Applying GOD's Principles." You will move *from Millstone to Milestone.*

In His service
Bob Marette
(Colossians 3:23-24)

1

The Three-Legged Stool

As I begin this book, it is important for me to ask you one question: Do *you* want to financially succeed? I can hear you mumbling now ... "Of course I do, that's why I got this book."

Well, I can guarantee your success. But before I talk about my guarantee, let me tell you about another guarantee. Back in 1999, a man named Ray Buchanan made a guarantee. He was a defensive back for the Atlanta Falcons, and he said, "I guarantee that the Falcons will beat the Denver Broncos in the Super Bowl." If we go back and check out history, we will see that, in fact, the Falcons lost that game. His guarantee was actually worthless. Let's go back to my guarantee. I can guarantee your success, because this is *not* my guarantee. Actually, it is God who is making the guarantee. If we read Joshua 1, verse 8, it states, "This book of the law [the Bible] will not depart from your mouth, but you shall meditate on it day and night and be careful to do according to everything that is written in it—for then you will make your way prosperous and then [listen to this] *you will have success.* " It doesn't say, you might have success, it says you *will* have success. If you can trust God in your lives, you know that His Word is true. When He says something, you know that you can count on it.

But, be careful! Success does not come from having the Bible on your nightstand. Success does not come from opening it up just on Sundays. Success does come from opening God's Word daily, meditating on God's Word daily, and obeying God's Word daily. I call it *meditate* and *do.* Prosperity and success come from not just partially obeying what God says. Partial obedience is actually disobedience. Let me say that again. Partial obedience is actually disobedience. Read James 2:10, which says, "For whoever keeps the whole law and yet stumbles in one *point,* he has become guilty of all."

Luke 9:23 states that we are to deny ourselves, and take up our cross *daily,* and follow Him. Denying ourselves is a big step toward contentment, which I will cover later. The Bible says we must be content. Let's act out of obedience and "do it." The Bible says to give and to give generously and cheerfully. Let's be faithful and do it. The Bible encourages us to get out of debt. Romans 13:8 reads, "Let no debt remain outstanding, except the continuing debt to love one another." Let's do it. Let's meditate on what God's Word says; then, let's act out of obedience.

The Bible goes on to say in many places that God owns it all. He owns not only our treasures, but our time and our talents as well. Additionally, He owns our families. Job pointed this out after he had lost his seven sons and three daughters. He stated, "Naked I came from my mother's womb, And naked I shall return there. The LORD gave and the LORD has taken away. Blessed be the name of the LORD." Additionally, the Bible says that God owns our body and that we were bought with a price.

Knowing that God owns everything—our treasure, our time, our talents, our family, our body—everything, we have a responsibility as stewards to use everything wisely. God expects us to use our time wisely. Are we doing it? God expects us to use our body in a pleasing manner. Are we doing it?

In Psalm 1:2-3, David says, "But his delight is in the law of the LORD, And in His law he meditates day and night. He will be like a tree *firmly* planted by streams of water, which yields its fruit in its season, And its leaf does not wither; And in whatever he does, *(get this)* he prospers."

Do you want success and prosperity? It's actually quite simple—meditate and do.

Whenever I teach the workshop, "How to Get Out of Debt in five to seven Years, Including Mortgage," many people come to learn the "secrets" of rapid debt elimination. However, I mention that debt elimination is only one leg of a three-legged stool. You may have seen this illustration before.

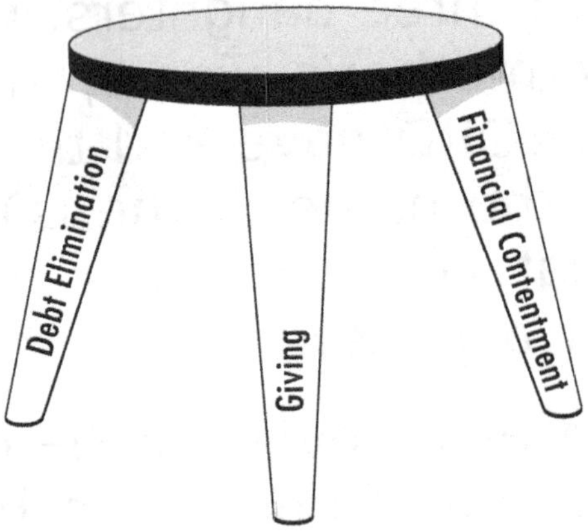

Every stool needs at least three legs to stand. If there are only two legs, the stool will collapse. This stool is no different. Without the other two legs, this stool also will collapse. This great debt-elimination plan of yours will collapse unless the other two areas are addressed.

What are these two other legs? They are financial contentment and giving. Without either one, the stool will collapse. If a person is not financially content, he or she will see that new "thing," and then decide that they must have it. I've got to get it and I've got to get it now, even if I have to spend the rest of my paycheck; even if I have to spend all my savings; and yes, even if I have to go into debt for it. If you are not financially content, that "want" or "the need to get" is so strong, that you will give in and get it, even though you cannot afford to pay cash for it. And so, the first leg crumbles.

If a person is not giving to the Lord's work, the Bible says that "want" will come upon him or her. Proverbs

11:24b states, "There is one who withholds what is justly due" (I take that to mean the tithe), "but it results only in want." Again, that "want" or "the need to get" is so strong that a person will buckle under its pressure. And so, the second leg crumbles.

If a person wants to get out of debt in five to seven years, including mortgage, he or she *must* get these first two principles into place. If you, the reader, cannot begin to see the need to make changes in your life in these two areas—financial contentment and giving—you might as well put this book down right now. You will be wasting your time. You will never get out of debt until you master these first two principles.

If you are not clear about what financial contentment and giving are, then keep reading. Over the next two chapters I will spell them out for you clearly so that you can make the necessary changes in your life so *you* can succeed.

2

Financial Contentment

When I teach the "Get Out of Debt in Five to Seven Years" workshop, I talk about the three-legged stool. Any stool needs at least three legs to stand, and this one is no different. Debt Elimination is only one leg. The other two legs are Financial Contentment and Giving. Let me tell you why I call these *critical.*

If a person is not financially content, there is *no way* he or she will ever get out of debt. I say that because that person sees something and without contentment, they want that new thing. They will get that new thing even if they have to spend their entire paycheck. They will get that thing even if they have to spend all their savings. They will get that new thing even if they have to go into debt. For many of us, the first requirement of getting out of debt—becoming financially content—is to get our "wanter" fixed.

Content is defined as "being satisfied with your lot, free from cares." The Bible talks a great deal about being content. In Philippians 4:11-12, Paul states, "I have learned to be content in whatever circumstances I am. I know how to get along with humble means, and I also know how to live in prosperity; in any and every circumstance I have learned the secret of being filled and going hungry, both of having abundance and suffering need." Paul at times had it all and at other times had very little, but in every situation, he was content. In I Timothy 6:7, Paul states, "For we have brought nothing into the world, so we cannot take anything out of it either."

Have you ever seen a hearse pulling a U-Haul? We cannot take anything with us. My question then becomes, if we cannot take anything with us, why do we spend so much of our time and effort and money trying to get *"stuff?"* Stuff that has no eternal value! Stuff that we will leave behind! Verse 8 then goes on to say, "If we have food and covering, with these we shall be content." We need food for the body, covering for the body (clothing) and covering for our heads (a roof). Let me ask you this: Do you have food and covering? If so, then you should be content. Hebrews 13:5 states, "Make sure that your character is free from the love of money, being content with what you have; for He Himself has said, *'I will never desert you, nor will I ever forsake you.'"*

Let me tell you what financial contentment is *not,* and then I will tell you what financial contentment *is.* Contentment is *not* when we focus on what we do not have. I wish I had that boat or motor home. I wish I had that new job. I wish my children went to that Christian school. If we are wishing, we are not content. We are not satisfied.

Contentment *is* when we focus on what we *do* have. Let me ask you: Have we as Americans been blessed? Of course we have. A pastor friend had just returned from a trip to India. He told me, "Bob, the people of India make the people of Old, Old Mexico look wealthy." Wow, that is hard to believe. We are a very rich material nation—two to three cars per household, a TV in every room, and a garage and basement full of stuff. But we as Americans have been blessed even greater because we have the freedom to openly read and discuss our Bible with others. There are many places around the world where the people do not have that freedom. We have Christian radio and television, as well as Christian bookstores. We have been blessed.

Let me ask you another question. Have we "as Christians" been blessed? Have we been blessed? *Yes.* Christ died for you and He died for me. If you and I call on the name of the Lord Jesus Christ, we will spend eternity with *Him* because of what He did for us. *There is no greater blessing!*

Let's not focus on all that we do not have. Do we have food, clothing, and shelter? Let's focus on that. Are we Americans? Let's focus on that. Are we saved by the blood of Jesus? Let's praise God and focus on that.

Contentment is *critical* as we strive to get out of debt. Without it we will fail. With it, we are well on our way to success.

3

Giving

I mentioned earlier about the three-legged stool. Any stool needs at least three legs to stand, and this one is no different. Debt Elimination is only one leg. The other two legs of our three-legged stool are Financial Contentment and Giving. In the last chapter, I talked about contentment, and now I want to give you what I consider to be *the key* to getting totally out of debt in a short period of time.

The second leg of the stool is Giving. I really see this as the key to getting totally out of debt because it brings the Lord into the middle of your finances. I previously discussed how financial contentment is critical, because if a person is not financially content, there is *no way* he or she will ever get out of debt. I say that because that person sees something and without contentment, they want that new thing. They will get that new thing even if they have to spend their entire paycheck, even if they have to spend all their savings, even if they have to go into debt.

Proverbs 11:24 states, "there is one who withholds what is justly due, (I take that to mean the tithe) and yet it results only in want." I believe if a person is not tithing, the result is financial discontent or "want," which, as I described, will keep a person deep in debt.

The Bible is very clear when it comes to giving. In Malachi, God says we are robbing Him if we do not bring the tithe to Him. Pastor Mike Ware in Denver tells me that many people are driving "stolen" cars and living in "stolen" houses, because we are taking the money we should be giving to God and using it to buy these things. When asked by a church member to pray for their finances, Pastor Mike always asks if the person is tithing. If the response is negative, then he asks the person, "So you want me to ask God to bless you with more finances so you can rob Him more?" Ouch! Do we trust God with our money, or do we not? If God commands us to give the tithe and we don't, we are like the fool who builds his house upon the sand. Matthew 7:26-27 states, "Everyone who hears these words of Mine and does *not* (emphasis added) act on them, will be like a foolish man who built his house on the sand. The rain fell, and the floods came, and the winds blew and slammed against that house; and it fell—and great was its fall." Jesus (God) has made His Word very clear in Scripture. We are to bring the tithe.

There is good news about God's commands to us regarding giving. In every case that I am aware of, when God commands us to give, He follows that command with a promise. Let's look at a few examples. In Proverbs 3:9-10, the writer says in verse 9, "Honor the Lord with your wealth and with the first of all your produce." Stop right there. God says He wants the first fruits of your labor and He commands us to give to Him. This is *not* a request. But verse 10 follows up with a promise—a conditional promise. He says, "then your barns will be filled with plenty and your vats will overflow with good wine." Wow, what a promise! But, like I said, this is a conditional promise. There are many unconditional promises in the Bible, and I am very grateful for them, but this one is conditional. God simply says, "If you will do verse 9, then I will do verse 10. If you give your first fruits to me, I will fill your barns." That is something I believe we all want.

Let's look at another example. Malachi 3:10 states, "Bring the whole tithe into the storehouse, so that there may be food in My house, and test Me now in this," says the LORD of hosts, "if I will not open for you the windows of heaven and pour out for you a blessing until it overflows." He says, "Bring the tithe." He doesn't say, "bring the tithe if you feel like it." This is a command. But He follows that command with a wonderful promise when He says He will open for you the windows of Heaven and pour out for you a blessing until it overflows.

Do you want that overflowing blessing? It is yours for the asking. Actually, it is yours for the doing. Bring the tithe and watch God work in your life. Not just in your financial life, but in your entire life, as well. It is critical, if you are trying to get out of debt, to be faithful in your giving. Do you really trust God?

Then, like the old hymn says, "Trust and Obey!" God has given to us and *commands* us to return a portion to Him. The good news is: 1) we get to keep 90 percent for ourselves, and 2) He follows His commands with wonderful promises of blessing.

We need to ask ourselves, "Why do we give?" Do we give because God needs the money? No, of course not. He owns it all anyway, right? He owns the cattle on a thousand hills; the silver is Mine and the gold is Mine, saith the Lord; the Earth is the Lord's and everything in it. We don't need to give for that reason because God does own it all. Let me ask you this: Do we give because the church needs the money? I know some are thinking *yes* and some are thinking *no.* I will be very clear. Do we give because the church needs the money? No—absolutely not. I will explain this more in a moment.

So, we don't give because God needs the money and we don't give because the church needs the money. Then, why do we give? I think Paul makes it very clear in Philippians 4:17, when he states, give to the ministry, "not that I seek the gift itself, but I seek for the profit which increases to your account." In Matthew 6:20, Jesus says, "But lay up for yourselves treasures in heaven, where neither moth nor rust destroys, and where thieves do not break in or steal." Howard Dayton in his book, *Your Money Counts,* states that every time you or I give to the Lord, it is like we are making a deposit into our account in the First National Bank of Heaven.[1] I think that very accurately reflects what happens when we give. Proverbs 19:17 states, "One who is gracious to a poor man lends to the LORD, and He will repay him for his good deed." Randy Alcorn, in his book, *The Treasure Principle,* puts it this way. "You cannot take it with you, but you can send it on ahead."[2]

Now, let me ask you again: Does the church need the money? Of course it does. But, that is not why we give. If God has called you to a certain church and said, "Give," and you don't give, here's what happens. God will bring someone else into your church who will give and then He will bless them instead of you. God has certain plans for your church and you can be part of the blessing or part of the problem. If you want God's blessing, you had better be obedient and give. We give out of obedience and as we give we will be blessed.

That brings up another question. What should our attitude be as we are giving? In II Corinthians 9:7, Paul says, "Each one must do just as he has purposed in his heart, not grudgingly or under compulsion, for God loves a cheerful giver." Did you know the word for cheerful comes from the root word that means "hilarious"? God loves a hilarious giver. Does that mean that as the plate is passed, we should get up and do cartwheels? I am not saying that. But, we should be doing cartwheels in our heart, saying, "God, you have blessed me tremendously. You have given me so much. I pray that you would take this money and multiply it and use it for your Kingdom." We should get excited, because, "Giving is a privilege." Being faithful in your giving will make it *so* much easier for you to get out of debt.

Let's back up one verse. In II Corinthians 9:6, Paul says, "he who sows sparingly will also reap sparingly, and he who sows bountifully will also reap bountifully." Do you want to reap sparingly? No, I didn't think so. Do you want to reap bountifully? Sure you do, and I do too. Then here is the answer. We need to sow bountifully.

Did you know the law of sowing and reaping is a law of God? It is a law of God, just like gravity is a law of God. I saw a bumper sticker that read, "God said it, I believe it, that settles it." Well, as good as that sounds, we can cross out the middle part. "God said it—that settles it—whether I believe it or not." Do you believe in gravity? If you don't, what impact will it have if you jump off a building, saying, "I don't believe in gravity"? There will be an impact, I can assure you of that. The law of sowing and reaping is the same. It works, whether we believe it or not. I heard someone once say, "As soon as God blesses me, then I will be a great giver." That is like a farmer who says, "God, as soon as you give me a great crop, *then* I will plant some seed." God already *has* blessed you tremendously. Look at what you have.

I've been asked many times if I sow financially, does that mean I will reap financially? Let me ask you—if you sow corn, will you get green beans. I believe God can choose any number of ways to bless us, and I also believe as we are faithful in our giving, (as well as the proper use of the other 90 percent), that God will bless us financially as a result of obedience. Let me say, however, that growing a crop is a long process and I cannot plant today and expect a one hundred-fold return tomorrow.

I have had people tell me that tithing does not work. When questioned further, they said, "Well we've been tithing for two weeks with no results. Tithing does not work." I want to caution each of you—If you are giving to get back, tithing will not work, because God doesn't look at the gift; He looks at the heart. He wants you to give cheerfully, obediently, and generously; not for the purpose of getting a return. Then *He will* open the windows and pour out a blessing until it overflows.

Are you trying to get out of debt, but finding it hard? It really can be quite simple. Be faithful with what God has already given you. Do you really want to reap bountifully? Then you have to sow bountifully. Start today.

One of my favorite radio teachers, Dr. John MacArthur, answered the question of why we give by stating it this way: "We give to God in order to get ... in order to give even more." Dr. MacArthur talked about an outward spiral. Picture a small spiral in the center, gradually getting bigger and bigger, then bigger and bigger still. On one side of the spiral is the Lord, and we are on the other side. He begins by giving us everything that we have. As we are faithful in giving back to Him, He not only gives us that same amount, but He will give us more. At this point, let me mention that many people give for this reason alone. These people say, "I am giving to God in order to get." However, that's not what God intended. As God increases what we are giving to Him, He expects us to increase what we are giving Him. When income increases for many people, they "increase their standard of living." We, as Christians, should not get caught up in this. As our income increases, we should instead "increase our standard of giving."

Let me tell you about two people you might have heard of over the years. Do you know the name R.G. LeTourneau? He developed the heavy earth-moving equipment in the early twentieth century, and became a very wealthy man. Let me give you another one. Do you know the name J.C. Penney? Many of us probably know that name too well. Did you know that both of these men, and there have been many others, in their final years of life were giving over 90 percent of their income to the Lord?

I want to ask you, "Would you like to give 90 percent of your income each month to the Lord?" Many of you are emphatically saying, "Yes." In the workshops that I teach, about 15–20 percent say, "Yes, I would like to do that." But my next question is the one that really matters. "Do you think you will ever be able to give 90% percent of your income to the Lord?" At the workshops, the number shrinks to a small few. What about *you?*

If you would like to give 90 percent, but do not think you ever will be able to, let me pose a scenario for you. Suppose God gives you a fantastic idea. You take the idea and develop it. Then you market it on the Internet, and suddenly your income grows to over one million dollars each year. (By the way, that is happening to many people these days.) Do you think that, by giving away 90 percent of your income to the Lord, you could live on $100,000 per year? Most of us might be able to squeak by. But let me be quick to say, the Lord is not going to give you that million-dollar idea if you are not faithful in the use of the money you have right now.

I have heard people say all the time, "If only I hit the Lotto, I would be a great giver." "If only I got that huge raise, then I would be a great giver." "If only I got that new job, then I would be a great giver." Let me say right up front. No, you wouldn't. Luke 16:10 states, "He who is faithful in a very little thing is faithful also in much; and he who is unrighteous in a very little thing is unrighteous also in much." If you have not been a good giver now, you wouldn't be if you had more. Let me tell you about two farmers who were talking one day. The first farmer says, "Charlie, if you had 10,000 sheep, would you give half of them to the Lord?" Charlie replies, "Yes, that would be exciting." The first farmer continues, "Charlie, if you had 5,000 cattle, would you give half of them to the Lord?" "Oh, but of course. It would be thrilling to give like that." Then comes the third question. "Charlie, if you had two pigs, would give one of them to the Lord?" After a long pause, Charlie gets angry and says, "That's not fair. You know I have two pigs." The question is not, "What would you do if...." The question actually is, "What are you currently doing with what you have in your pocket right now." Are you being faithful with what you have?

The word "tithe" literally means "tenth," or 10 percent, which is one-tenth. There are many Christian scholars who disagree on whether we need to tithe, or "give as God directs." I have heard well-meaning people say that tithing is an Old Testament principle, to which I reply, "so are the Ten Commandments." I personally believe that the tithe is a good place to start, and it (the 10 percent) is the floor and we should increase from there.

As you are reading this book, I am going to assume that you already are giving to the Lord with your tithes and offerings. However, I know that you have friends who are not tithing, but would like to. I used to talk about two plans for your friend to choose from: Plan A and Plan B. Plan A is *the* place for your friend to start. *It is God's best.* Today, you tell your friend to "start tithing." Share with him or her what Scripture says about tithing. Tell them how God has blessed you for being obedient to tithe. Share how others have been blessed as well. Your friend *must* start tithing today. *It is God's best plan.*

Some of your friends, however, will resist, saying, "I cannot afford to tithe." It's up to you to tell them, "Friend, you cannot afford *not* to tithe." They *can* afford to tithe; their faith is just weak at this time. At this point I *used to* talk about Plan B. Very simply, Plan B said to start today at 2 percent; then in three months increase to 4 percent; then after six months increase to 6 percent; after nine months, increase to 8 percent, and then, after one year, increase to 10 percent, a tithe.

However, a pastor challenged me on this. He indicated that during that first three months, when a person was giving 2 percent, they were only being 20 percent obedient. It would be like a father telling his son to milk the cows for the next ten days, and the son said, "Okay, Dad, I will milk them, but only for two days." Let me say something again that you must share with your friends. "Partial obedience is disobedience." Hear it again, because this is so important: "Partial obedience is disobedience." There is no Plan B. Plan A—God's Best—is the only plan. Begin tithing now.

I talked with another pastor recently who thought the 2 percent, 4 percent, etc. plan was a good plan because he said some people cannot afford to tithe. I personally think that many people use this 2 percent plan to justify keeping their cable television, or their new car, or their luxurious lifestyle, and that they could "easily" afford to tithe by making a few lifestyle adjustments. This is part of the behavioral changes I will be discussing throughout this book. Okay, here's the deal. This is critical. This is for you who have been tithing all along. I have met many people who have been tithing for the last twenty years, and when I shared this, they really felt convicted by the Holy Spirit to make a change.

Don't stop at 10 percent.

I have read through the Bible many times, and I have never read, "Thou shalt not give more than 10 percent." The Bible does not say that. It does say that we should give as God has prospered us. Remember, as our income goes up, it should be our standard of giving that increases—not our standard of living.

How do you think R.G. LeTourneau and J.C. Penney were giving 90 percent of their income to the Lord? Did they start at 10 percent, and then the Lord opened the floodgates and their businesses multiplied and they started giving 90 percent? I know the Lord is more than able to do that, and in some cases He may. But in the case of Mr. LeTourneau and Mr. Penney, they started at 10 percent, went to 12 percent, then 15 percent, then 18 percent, then 22 percent, etc. Each step of the way, the Lord continued opening the doors and increasing their income. Remember the "outward spiral." God gave more to them (and gives more to us) in order that they might give more still.

I would ask you *right now* to set the book aside for a few moments. Come before the Lord and ask Him what you should do. Should you increase to 12 percent? Should you increase to 15 percent? Should you increase to 20 percent? After you have asked the Lord, then be quiet and listen to His response. This is the easy part. The hard part is, after you have heard from the Lord, be obedient to what the Spirit of God is telling you to do. (At a workshop in Nebraska recently, one man responded that God was leading him and his wife to increase to 25 percent in total giving. He thought he was doing well, but realized that God could do even more through them. This couple has just recently increased to 35 percent.)

Over the years, I have heard many, many people claim, "I cannot afford to tithe." I would like to encourage you that I believe you cannot afford *not* to tithe." People say, "I do not have the 10 percent to give." When I hear that, I ask them, "When you get paid, what percent of income do you have?" The answer is obviously 100 percent. They have 10 percent, because they have 100 percent to start with. They don't think they can give because they usually put off giving until everything else is paid. They *must* give the tithe right off the top. I have found that it is easier to give 10 percent to the Lord when I have 100 percent, rather than pay all my bills and then try to take 10 percent out of the 11 percent that's left. I believe God knew we would feel that way, and that is one reason why He says to give *first.*

I have a question that I have asked thousands of times to folks who are not tithing, and every time the response is always the same. The question in the chart below is—where would *you* rather be?

You	You & God
100 percent	90 percent

Would you rather have 100 percent of your income to work with, or would you rather have 90 percent of your income for you and God to work with?

The truth is, if you are not tithing, God is not in your financial life. Let me put it this way: Ninety percent of our income "*with* God's blessing" will go further than 100 percent of our income "*without* God's blessing." If you are not tithing right now, I am certain you feel you could use a pay raise. Let me tell you how to get that pay raise—start tithing. I know it may not be clear as to how God works, but I have heard testimony after testimony of people who were struggling to make ends meet, then they started tithing (trusting God), and somehow God worked in their lives and provided above and beyond their needs.

I believe Scripture is also clear that God can enable us to avoid many of those costly emergencies, if He is involved in our finances. If He is not, though, I believe those emergencies will find us and keep us in financial troubles. Tithing brings God's protection on our finances. I will discuss this further when we talk about emergencies.

Here is another verse that might already be familiar to you. Proverbs 3:5 tells us to do something and to not do something. It states, *do* "trust in the Lord with all your heart." Part of our trust in the Lord is recognizing that He owns everything. Since He has commanded us to give back to Him, we can trust Him to meet our needs when we do. Our trust in the Lord by tithing is reflected through our obedience.

The verse continues though, by telling us, "*Do not* lean on your own understanding." When we say we cannot afford to tithe, we are leaning on our own understanding. This reflects our disobedience. Remember what I said earlier: partial obedience is disobedience.

Let me wrap up this chapter with a Scripture verse and a question. Deuteronomy 14:23(b) in The Living Bible states what the purpose of tithing is. It simply states, "The purpose of tithing is to teach you to always put God first in your life." My question to you is, "Is God first in your life?" And be honest with yourself. He either is or He is not.

After you have answered this question, you can move toward getting out of debt. Let me caution you, if you are not willing to become content and become faithful in your giving, stop right now. Ask the Lord to help you in these areas. You can do it, with His help. However, if you choose not to, I believe you will never get out of debt. You might as well put this book down right now, because you will be wasting your time by reading it.

But since you have decided to secure the first two legs of our "three-legged stool," keep reading. It will bring "the *light of hope* to the darkness of debt," and you will be "challenged, encouraged, and equipped to become good stewards of God's resources." It will bring you *from a millstone* (of debt) *to a milestone* (of *freedom* from debt).

[1] Howard Dayton, Your Money Counts. Gainesville, GA, 1996 Crown Financial Ministries, page 76.

[2] Randy Alcorn, The Treasure Principle, Sisters, OR, Multnomah Publishers, 2001 page 17

4

Debt: What? Why? How?

Now that I have addressed the critical, foundational principles of *financial contentment* and *giving,* now, and only now can, we begin to talk about getting out of debt. As I mentioned earlier, if you are not willing to become content financially and if you are not giving to the Lord, there is *no way* that you will ever get out of debt. But I know you have made the decision to accomplish these first two legs of our stool, so let's proceed to the third leg of our stool—debt elimination.

Before we get too far into our discussion, it is important to define what debt actually is. Webster defines *debt* as "a sin or trespass, a state of owing, something owed, an obligation." I want to say right up front that I do not consider debt to be a sin. Many times, in talking with pastors, they do not want me to come to tell the people that they are in sin if they are in debt. I do not believe that to be. "A state of owing, something owed, an obligation:" that is what I will be talking about throughout this book.

I want to develop the definition a little and add that a debt is something that can be paid off. Things like utility bills, rent, taxes, and insurance are not debts, because they can never be paid off. Rather, they are to be considered as expenses that occur on a periodic basis. Every month, the expense is incurred, then paid, and then incurred again and then paid again. The only way to eliminate paying for these items is to eliminate the items from your daily lives.

I want also to tell you what debt is. *Debt is debt is debt.* I just shake my head when I watch ex-athletes on TV saying things like, "Let me help you get out of debt by getting this new loan, or a new mortgage, or a consolidation loan." Let me say it again. *Debt is debt is debt.* I know these people were pretty good athletes in their days, but either they are terrible business people, or they are just trying to earn a few bucks, or they are just plain ignorant. A loan is a debt; a mortgage loan is a debt; and a consolidation loan is a debt. One more time—*debt is debt is debt.*

Okay, so we are going to "Get Out of Debt Using God's Principles." The best place to look as we begin our discussion of debt is in God's Word—the Holy Bible. One scripture verse that we have all heard over the years is Romans 13:8, which states, "Owe nothing to anyone except the continuing debt to love one another." Is that a prohibition to borrowing? Does that mean we should never have any kind of debt? I believe it simply is a warning to us, because debt affects relationships.

Let me illustrate: Do you have someone at work or in your neighborhood who seems to waste your time? Someone who is constantly bothering you? Do you know how to lovingly get rid of a person like that? It's easy! *Loan them some money!* You heard me right: Loan them some money. If that person is unable to repay you at the designated time, what will happen? You guessed it. They will avoid you. The reason simply is: debt affects relationships. It affects relationships between neighbors, between co-workers, between friends, between parent and child. If you have ever owed any person some money, or someone has owed it to you, you know how it can affect the relationship. However, debt really affects the relationship between ourselves and our heavenly Father.

Proverbs 22:7 states, "The rich rules over the poor, and the borrower *becomes* the lender's slave," or servant. Do you know what a servant is? It is a person who goes to work during the day—works hard all day long, then comes home, fixes a meal, goes to bed, and gets up to begin all over again. Does that sound familiar to anyone? Sure, you say, but I get a paycheck. Do you really? If you are like most people, when you get that paycheck, there is a line of people wanting a part of your check. Hopefully, you have allowed the Lord to be at the front of the line. Uncle Sam has already taken his portion. But then there is the mortgage banker, the grocer, the car dealer, the insurance man, the creditors, and so on. There are usually more people in line than there is money to go around. That's what I call, "having month at the end of the money." You have worked hard over the last two weeks and you get paid. After paying your bills, your response is probably, "Gosh, where did it all go." You have put in your forty to sixty hours a week, just to send it out to all your creditors. Doesn't that make you feel like a slave?

If you are like many people, you think, "That's not fair, I worked hard, I deserve a break today." So, you go out and enjoy life with plastic, thinking you will only do that until you get that raise. But the raise doesn't come and you continue with the plastic. Eventually the raise does come, but you have increased your monthly outgo to the point that you must still use the plastic for those enjoyable things in life.

Let's take a look at another verse. In Matthew 6:24, Jesus states, "No one can serve two masters; for either he will hate the one and love the other, or he will be devoted to one and despise the other. You cannot serve God and wealth." Another version says, "You cannot serve God and money." I have heard people over the years say, "Well, I can do it. I can serve both God and money." Well, excuse me, but the Bible says you cannot.

Let me put this verse in English for you today. In Colorado, we all know the name Terrell Davis, former running back for the Denver Broncos and Super Bowl MVP. I want you to picture Terrell Davis standing on the fifty-yard line with the ball tucked under his arm, ready to run to the end zone. However, one end zone is marked "God" and the other is marked "Money." I don't care how good Terrell Davis was, and he was good. I don't care how strong he was, how fast he was, or how much money he was earning. There is no way that he could run to both end zones. Either he is running toward "God" or he is running toward "Money." If he is running toward "Money," what is he doing? That's right, he is running away from "God". The same is true for you and me. If we are running toward "Money" we cannot be running toward God. You cannot serve two masters. But, remember the earlier verse. Proverbs 22:7 says, "The borrower is *servant* to the lender.

As you continue through this book, I will provide a lot of answers, as well as a lot of encouragement. However, for right now I have some *bad news.* If a person is in debt, he or she, according to Proverbs 22:7, is servant to the lender. But according to Matthew 6:24, he or she cannot serve two masters. I believe the Bible is very clear in stating that if you have any debt that you cannot pay off right now, even a mortgage, then there is *no way* you can be a 100 percent bondservant to Jesus Christ. That really breaks my heart.

Have you ever heard someone say, "I believe God wants me to go on this mission trip, but I cannot afford to go"? I have heard people say, "God called me into a ministry full-time, but I cannot quit my job. I have to pay toward all my debts." If all you had was a mortgage and God called you to go on a long-term mission trip, you probably could not go, because you would have to try to sell the house, which could take a long time, or you would have to find someone to take over payments, which is easier said than done. If you had no debt and you owned your home, and then God calls, you can say, "Here am I, Lord, send me." All you need to do is to find someone to house-sit while you are gone, which would probably take ten minutes.

Now for the *good news!* In the following chapters, I have a plan for you to show you how to get rid of all your debt in a short period of time, typically five to seven years, including your mortgage. In some cases, it might be two to three years. In other cases, it might be eleven or twelve years. But let me ask you this. Is eleven or twelve years better than twenty-eight or twenty-nine years, where you are right now? This is a plan that *will* work, *if* you want it to. Do you want to continue to be a bondservant to the creditors or to the Lord Jesus Christ? The choice is yours.

Next, let's address *why* we are in debt. As we discussed earlier, one of the main reasons we are in debt is that we have *not* been content. Let me put that into language that might be a little more clear. We are in debt because we are consumers rather than stewards. A consumer wants things now. It's called "instant gratification." I have to get that "thing" right now, because that is the way we have been taught to buy. A consumer will spend more money now—money that he does not have—to get that new item right away. Here is what happens. You have heard this before. A person will spend money he doesn't have to get things he doesn't need to impress people he doesn't even like.

Let me tell you what a steward does. A steward will pay cash for everything. If the money is not available now, he will wait until the money is there, and then he will pay cash for that item. Wow! What a concept! My parents used to call that "layaway." Today, it could be called "delayed gratification." But delayed gratification is a term that is foreign to most of us, because, "I have to have it now." By the way, as a person buys things with cash, sometimes he will be able to get a better deal. I want to share with you another new concept. Most places still accept cash. But as you use cash, you are going against what everyone else is doing. But that's okay, because everyone else is broke.

Now, let's address the issue of *how* we got into debt. I have people call me all the time with a long list of their debts and they wonder how it all happened. They have a good income, but there just isn't anything left at the end of the month. In fact, in many cases, there is still month left at the end of the money.

The way a person gets into a situation is actually very easy. It's called the Monthly Payment Trap, and we will talk more about that in a later chapter. People get a job, have a good salary, and then start spending, because "I owe it to myself." They buy a few little things that only cost $20 per month. Then they get a cell phone at $39 per month. Then comes a gym membership at $40 per month. Then a computer follows, and it's only $75 a month. Then comes a time share, and hey, it's real attractive and we can use it on vacation, and it's only $125 a month. Then, after a nice raise, she "deserves" a new car, and it's only $350 per month. But he has been working hard too, and so he gets that new truck, and it's "only" $475 per month. Now it's time to move, because we don't want to rent, and the new house is only $300 more each month than renting, so now they are paying $1,450 (plus another $300 for escrow payments), and then they need furniture for the new house, and the new sofa, chairs, big screen TV, etc., is only $200 a month. Do you see what has happened here? Every decision was easy, because it was "only 'x' dollars per month," and hey, we can afford that. The way a hole is dug is one shovelful at a time, and one little shovelfull of dirt is not that much. We can handle that. Let me just say, the Monthly Payment Trap is just that—a trap that will ensnare you. Now you feel like a slave.

Does that sound like you? Are you tired of being a slave? The answer is as easy as 1-2-3.

1) Put the credit cards away. Cut them *all* up. You do not need them. All they do is give you an idea that you can afford something because of the small

monthly payment. (I can hear the groans and the justifications beginning. We will address those later.)

2) After you get paid, make sure you have put the Lord at the front of the line. Be faithful in your giving.

3) Be diligent in the use of the remaining 90 percent.

Be content with what you have. If you are not, I can guarantee you will not be successful financially and you will not be a successful Christian—serving and giving of yourself to your church and to others. But if you keep reading with an open mind, and apply the easy steps, you will be freed from the slavery—the bondage—and now you will be free to serve. You will move from a *millstone to a milestone.*

5

The Roadmap

As we begin the journey to become debt-free, and thus "free," we must lay out a plan—a roadmap. Most people operate without a roadmap with their finances, and the results are disastrous. You have heard the saying, and it is really true: if you fail to plan, you simply plan to fail. If you don't know where you are going, any road will take you there. We all start out with great ideas of what we want to accomplish: start our own business; become a millionaire by age forty; travel the world. However, because we have failed to plan, life happens to us and we begin to dig a hole for ourselves. One by one, our goals and dreams begin to fall by the wayside. As Thoreau stated, we live those lives of "quiet desperation." The hole gets deeper and deeper, and eventually we think, "Gosh, I hope I can just make it."

The roadmap you need is made up of four parts. First, you need to know "where are you?" That's Point A. Next, you want to determine "where do you want to go?" That's Point B. Third, the roadmap shows you "how to get from where you are to where you want to go." How do you get from Point A to Point B? Let me just pause and say that this is what every financial counselor does when he/she sits down with a client.

These three steps are important, but I believe they are worthless, unless the fourth step is considered. That step is simply, "What is keeping you from getting to Point B?" "Why are you not already at Point B?" "Why are you not on your way to point B?" You see, most of us are stuck on Point A where we were ten, twenty, or thirty years ago. It is at this point that we need to discuss behavior.

Where Are You?

Too many times, people say the first step is to determine where you want to go. This is not the obvious first step, and let me illustrate why. I live in Denver. If someone asks me how to get to Kansas City, I say, "Get on Interstate 70 and go east." However, I say that because I *know* that I am in Denver. If someone wanted to go to Kansas City and they lived in Washington, D.C., they don't want to go east. Now, they could get to Kansas City from Washington, D.C. by going east, but they would go a long, long way before getting there. They would travel about 24,000 miles to make a trip that should only be 1,000 miles. Many people do that with their finances, because they do not know where they are financially. They have buried themselves in debt, and yet they think, "I need to start investing for the future." Wait! You have to know where you are before you can decide where you want to go.

The Bible says that you should "know well the condition of your flocks and pay attention to your herds." (Proverbs 27:23) Now, most of us don't have flocks or herds, but we do have other assets (house, cars, furniture, "stuff"). The Bible says we should know what we have. And we, as Christians, know that God owns it all and we are merely stewards of His resources. However, I believe that knowing the condition should not be limited to our assets, but to our liabilities, as well. I classify assets and liabilities as, "What does God own?" and "What do I owe?" See Appendix A for a form that you can use to truly "know well your condition." It is simply referred to as a Net Worth Statement.

The first step in trying to get out of debt is ask yourself, "What is my current situation? How deep is the hole that I have dug?" I want to warn you, in many cases, this can be a real eye-opener. I make available to people at my workshops a form that can be used to list their debts. On it, I have ten lines for the debts. More than once (many more times than once) has someone said, "I need more space." I have seen people with more than twenty-five debts. In some cases there are small debts, just a lot of them. In most cases, however, there are many large debts. The comment I receive all the time is that "putting my debts down on paper was the best thing I have ever done, because now I know just how bad the situation is." Often people say it isn't nearly as bad as they had suspected. Let me say, you *must* know the starting point as you begin this journey that will lead you out of bondage and into freedom.

Another part of knowing where you are, in addition to knowing how deep the hole is that you dug, is knowing what it will take for you to not only get out of the hole, but to begin saving in a manner that will enable you to get where you really want to be. As I proceed through this step, I want to warn you. This *will* open your eyes to the fact that you need to change the way you are currently spending your money. This is a very simple step to follow, as we are only looking at "what" you need to be doing. Later on in the book, I will address the tougher part: "how" you are going to do it.

The question I want to ask you right now is this: "If you were to retire today, how much money would you want coming in each and every year, in terms of today's dollars." Would you want $20,000 per year? Would you want $50,000 per year? Would you want $80,000 per year? As you ask this question, you might subtract what you know you already have. If you "know" that your company will provide a monthly lifetime pension of $1,600 each month (that's almost $20,000 per year), and your goal is to have $50,000 per year, then your additional need would be approximately $30,000 ($50,000 minus the $20,000 from your pension). If you have other assets that will pay an income, you can subtract that income from the desired income as well.

Let me tell you what I have found over many years of teaching and counseling. Most people do not have anything in the way of assets that can be used to provide an income. There are really only two places where most Americans have any assets, and that is in the 401(k) plan at work as well as in the equity in their home. The reason this is the case is simple. A monthly decision does not have to be made to make their house payment, so the loan goes down (a small amount each month, but it does go down) and so equity increases. In many parts of the country, houses will appreciate, giving more equity to the homeowner. Again, a decision is not made each month in order for the house to appreciate.

Regarding the 401(k), the funds are automatically withdrawn from the paycheck before you see it, and so, the value of the 401(k) increases. Again a decision is not required each month as to whether or not you will invest into the plan. You make that decision once each year during open enrollment, and then it happens automatically. By the way, this is the best way to invest—automatically—because you do not miss what you do not see.

As a result, many people have built up some assets in these two places. However, the government, in their infinite wisdom, has now enabled us to withdraw these funds. We can now take out a second mortgage, and hey, the interest is tax-deductible. Now you can get all that "stuff" we talked about earlier, and, you guessed it, it comes with a monthly payment. Also, the government has now allowed, in many situations, for you to borrow from your 401(k) plan. Again, it comes with a monthly payment plan to pay it back. But there is a scenario that is even worse. The government has tried to restrict you from withdrawing money from your 401(k) plan by making you pay taxes on this money. They have tried to deter you from this by penalizing you additionally. However, many Americans, and maybe even you, have paid the price and pulled funds out for this neat "stuff." So, in most cases, there are no assets to provide income which can reduce the amount that we want at retirement.

Using the following chart, come down the left-hand column and find the dollar amount that you would want coming in at your retirement. I often hear the question, "Does that mean *if* I am debt free?" I am hoping that the person would be debt free by retirement age, but this portion of the plan is just their income desire. If you would like $50,000 per year coming in at retirement, because you have a lot of debt, but you think you could "get by" on $40,000 with no debt, *and* you plan to get totally out of debt, then by all means use the $40,000 income level.

The next step is to go across the top of the chart and determine how many years remain between now and the time you will retire. Let me say at this point: retirement does not necessarily have to be age sixty-five. It could be fifty-five, or it could be seventy-five. This is your plan. Some say that they "never" want to retire, but they want to work until they drop. (By the way, that is exactly how I feel. I want to teach and write and encourage and challenge and equip until the day I leave this Earth.) If this is the case, you should determine at what age do you want to be able to "financially" retire, not having to work. Let's assume you are forty years old right now. (I can hear some of you saying, "Man, that's old," and I can hear others say, "I cannot remember that far back. I wish I were forty again.") For purposes in this book, I will use the example of a forty-year old person who wants to retire at age sixty-five, and wants $50,000 of income each year. That means he or she has twenty-five years to save up to get that lump sum of $834,000, which is needed to generate $50,000. (If $834,000 were generating a return of 6 percent, that would provide an annual income of $50,040, each and every year.)

Table A

Monthly Savings Required to Reach Your Financial Freedom Goal

Annual Income Goal (in today's $$)	Approx. Nest Egg Needed (in today's $$)	Monthly Savings Needed to Reach Your Financial Freedom Goal						
		Years Remaining Until Financial Freedom						
		40 years	35 years	30 years	25 years	20 years	15 years	10 years
$10,000	$167,000	$88	$125	$182	$267	$400	$633	$1,101
20,000	334,000	175	250	363	533	799	1,263	2,197
30,000	500,000	262	375	544	799	1,198	1,894	3,295
40,000	667,000	350	501	726	1,066	1,599	2,527	4,396
50,000	834,000	437	626	907	1,331	1,997	3,157	5,492
60,000	1,000,000	527	751	1,088	1,598	2,397	3,788	6,590
70,000	1,167,000	613	876	1,270	1,865	2,797	4,421	7,691
80,000	1,334,000	700	1,001	1,451	2,130	3,196	5,051	8,787
90,000	1,500,000	787	1,126	1,632	2,397	3,595	5,682	9,886
100,000	1,667,000	875	1,251	1,814	2,663	3,995	6,313	10,984

Now you know that you want $50,000 per year and you know that you have twenty-five years to save. At this point, you simply go across the row at $50,000 to the right, and you go down the twenty-five years column. Where these two lines intersect, it will tell you what you need to be saving. In this instance, the $50,000 row and the twenty-five-year column intersect at $1,331. That means to save the $834,000 needed to provide the $50,000 annual income over the next twenty-five years, you must save $1,331. Are you sitting down right now? You need to save that $1,331 each and every ... month. That's right. Every month you need to be saving a big (rather a *huge*) chunk of change.

At the workshops that I teach, I ask the question, "How many of you" (in a class of 100 to 200) "can save the amount you have determined?" Let me just say, I almost never see a hand. If a person could save that kind of money each month, they would not be attending a workshop on how to get out of debt. There are better things to do on a given Saturday morning than to attend a workshop, but nearly all of the attendees are there because they cannot even begin to save what they need.

NOTE: *The Approximate Nest Egg Needed* assumes that you can get a 6 percent return on an "income" fund to generate the *Annual Income Goal* desired. The *Monthly Savings Needed to Reach Your Financial Freedom Goal* assumes an average 3 percent inflation and 10 percent annual return on savings during investment period. The monthly investment amounts will actually produce a higher accumulated asset amount than shown in the *Approximate Nest Egg Needed* in the second column, because of the inflation factor of 3 percent. These figures are not intended to be a projection of any investment results, and no assurance of any level of investment return can be provided.

At this point, I can hear the sighs of the seminar attendees, and I can even hear your sighs right now. "Yikes," you say. "I am really in trouble." Well, you are right. You *are* in trouble. Unless you make some changes right now, you will always be in serious trouble.

Where Do You Want to Go?

Now that you have determined just how bad the situation really is, it's time to figure out your final destination. Where is it you really want to go? What do you want to accomplish financially? I recommend that a person (or a couple) sit down and make a list of what he/she (they) want to accomplish. In the event of a couple, I recommend that they individually make a list, then compare it and consolidate it. What may be *very* important to one may be of little importance to the other. They need to decide at this point if this is something that is important to them, as a couple. In some cases, one might say it's not really that important for *us* to accomplish my goal. In other cases, the other spouse might feel, "If it's really that important to my spouse, then it really is important to me as well."

As you are making the list of what you want to accomplish, I want you to begin again to dream. Ask yourself, "If I had all the time and money in the world, what would I do with my life?" Okay, I know you are probably thinking I have lost it and am playing the "name it and claim it" game. Rest assured, I am not. "Name it and claim it" says that if I just tell God that I want it, and "claim" it as mine, then God is obligated to give it to me. By doing this, a person is making God a genie that grants wishes. That is not what I am doing here. I want you to ask yourself, "If I had all the time and money in the world, what would I do with my life?"

I want you to resuscitate those dreams you had when you started out on your own. Did you want to travel the world? Did you want to go on that long-term mission trip? Did you want to go on that Alaskan cruise? If you had all the time and money in the world, what would you do with your life? What would you do? By the way, it would take all the time *and* all the money to be able to accomplish these things. Some people have all the time in the world, but have no money. Others have all the money in the world, but they are working one hundred hours each week. Remember, if you fail to plan, you are planning to fail. You need to set some goals and have some dreams before you can accomplish them.

Let me share a few things on my list. If I had all the time and money in the world, my wife and I would build a large ranch house in the mountains with a great view of Pikes Peak. The house would have plenty of room for our kiddos and grandchildren to stay. In one end, it would have a recording studio so I could do a daily call-in radio show from home.

Another item on my list is I would work hard on improving my golf game. Those people who know me and know my golfing abilities would be the first to tell you that it would take all the time and all the money in the world to help my golf game, but I would like to try.

The favorite item on my list is that I would want to give more to God's work. I am currently giving time, talent, and treasure to my church and several other organizations, but if I had all the time and money in the world, I would give time, talent, and treasure to these and to many others. I want to be one who gives over 90 percent of my income to the Lord's work.

After you have determined where you are financially, now it's time to dream and determine where you want to go. As you do this, dream *big.* Remember, these are *your* goals and you need to know where you want to go before you can get there.

Before we leave this area, it is important to ask another question. *What exactly is a goal?* I ask this question, and the typical response is a target, something to aim at, something you want to accomplish. In my opinion, there are three key elements to every goal. First, a goal is a dream. You have a dream that you want to accomplish. It is important to you. It may be the purpose for your life. It may be a driving force. Whatever it might be, it is something that you really want.

Let's take this one step further. A goal is a dream with a deadline. Your goal must have a time limit attached to it. You want to accomplish something and you want to do it in a certain time period. A dream with a deadline. That's important. But also, a goal is a dream with a deadline and a written plan of action. You must know how you are going to accomplish something, and it must be written. If it is something that you just hope to get, with no real time frame and no real plan of action, it is not a goal. It is just pie in the sky. Remember this as you are writing down your goals. A goal is a dream with a deadline and a written plan of action. Let me illustrate the importance of goals with a story that you might have heard previously.

In 1953, the graduating class of Yale University was surveyed, and it turned out that only 3 percent left school with written goals. In 1973, twenty years later, those same graduates were found and resurveyed, and it turns out that the 3 percent who left school with written goals were worth more financially than the 97 percent combined. Now I want to ask you this. Were the 97 percent a bunch of dummies? I mean, we are talking Yale University here. But let me tell you that you can go to any college campus and find the same thing. Three to four percent will leave school with goals and 96–97 percent will not. The question at this point is: Will *you* develop goals? Remember, a goal is a "dream, with a deadline, and with a written plan of action." If you want to be in the 3–4 percent of the people who succeed financially, you *must* develop goals, write them down, and put a timeline to it.

How do you get from here to there?

"How do I get from where I am right now to where I really want to be?" The rest of this book will answer this question, as well as the last question, "What is keeping me from getting to that point?" Now that you have your current situation located, and now that you know where you want to go, it's time to start planning your trip. The way to get to your destination is really quite simple. There are three easy steps that we will cover in the next chapter. I say easy, because they are easy—if you really want to accomplish your goals. Those three steps are simply:

1) No new debt

Sounds easy enough, doesn't it? (You are probably saying right now, it's *not* easy because I will always have debt payments.) Let me assure you, it *is* easy, and we will see just how easy it is when we get there.

2) Piggyback

This simply means when we get debt #1 paid off, we take those funds and apply them to the next debt #2. Debt #2 will be paid off faster, because of the extra money being applied. Once it is paid off, now we take all the funds we were paying to debt #1 and the funds we were paying to debt #2 and add them to what we have been paying to debt #3. We keep "piggybacking" the funds from previous debt payments to the current debt. This will get the average American out of debt in about nine to eleven years, including the mortgage.

3) Accelerate

To accelerate, we simply find extra money in our budget and add that to the entire process. This accelerates the process to get the average American out of debt in about five to seven years, including the mortgage. This is simple as you will see later, even though right now you are saying, "There's no way!" Keep reading and you will discover just how simple it is.

These three steps will get you out of debt quickly and will get you to the point where you can start a serious investment program. You will build wealth quickly, because you will have *no* debt to slow you down.

What is keeping you from reaching your goals?

In order to accomplish the three simple steps above, we are going to have to address some behavioral changes. I want to tell you upfront, this process is all about change. This process will be simple, but it might be a little uncomfortable. I want to warn you that to accomplish your goals, you need to continue through this book.

I also want to warn you that what you will read will only be 20 percent knowledge. You will not learn a lot of new ideas here. This is just plain common sense information. These common sense ideas are what your grandparents took for granted. They just knew these were the best things to do. So if only 20 percent is knowledge, what's the other 80%? You guessed it! Behavior. Eighty percent of what I'll be telling you relates to changes in your behavior. If you want to be successful, you have *got* to make changes.

There are two pieces of good news that I want to share with you that will keep you going. First, I am not going to tell you that you need to live like a pauper or a hermit while you are going through this process. I am not going to cut all the fun out of your life. You can still enjoy life and become successful at the same time. It *will* take some diligence and some discipline, two words that are foreign to many in the U.S. today.

The second bit of good news is, this is all about your making choices. Throughout this book, I will make many recommendations that might seem contrary to anything you have ever heard before. I am going to tell you to "go right," when all you have been taught over the years is to "go left." You might say, "Bob, I have never heard of that before." Let me ask you, does that make my way wrong? You might also say, "Bob, all my friends are going left." Let me ask you this: "Are all your friends financially successful?" I am saying, "Go right!"

Whenever I do a workshop, and as I continue throughout this book, I know there will be several places where some people will fold their arms, slide back in their chair, and look at me as if I am crazy. That's okay. Like I said, it's all about you making choices. If I say "go right" ten times, and you say, "Bob, I'll go right eight times, but these two times, I am going to keep going left," that's okay. If you "go right" one time, I will feel like I have had an impact in your life.

But let me ask you, please, do not shut your mind to my way, just because it seems weird. Keep an open mind and give it a try. If it doesn't work, go back to doing things your way. But, I can assure you, it *will* work. It already has for thousands.

Well, there's your roadmap to success. I would recommend that you stop reading right now, and, if you are married, get with your spouse, and figure out the first two steps of the roadmap. Where are you right now? Ask, "How deep is that hole that we have dug for ourselves?" Next, make a list of all the things that you want to achieve, individually and as a couple. If you do these first two steps together, I can assure you that you are on your way to *getting rid of that millstone* around your neck and you are on your way *to the milestone* of getting totally out of debt in a short period of time.

6

Three Simple Steps

I mentioned in the last chapter that once you have a handle on your current situation (Where Are You?), and once you and your spouse have made written goals (Where Do You Want to Go?), then it is time for the challenge (How Do You Get From Here to There?). I say it is a challenge, because if it were easy, everyone would be doing it. The truth is, it is going to take some work, some hard work, but the rewards will be well worth the time and effort (and pain) to get there.

The way you get from where you are (under the weight of a *millstone* of debt) to where you want to be (the *milestone* of being totally debt free and beginning to accumulate wealth) will challenge you and your present thinking, but it can be accomplished. I say there are Three Simple Steps to get from here to there. They are simple steps, but they require something that may not be quite so simple: desire and discipline.

Desire is critical. Let me say desire is *not*—"Oh, it sure would be nice to get out of debt, and I am hoping that it is going to happen." Listen closely: if that's how you are approaching this, I can guarantee that it will *never* happen. That's right, it will *never, never, never* happen. In order to get out of debt, you have got to want it so bad you can taste it. You have got to want it so bad that you are willing to make some changes in the way you live each day—in the way you spend money each day. Now, like I have said before, I am not asking you to live like a pauper and make massive, drastic changes (although if you decided you wanted to, this whole process would happen even faster). I am saying that you will need to decide where you want to make changes. I am going to recommend that you not make massive drastic changes, but that you make many little changes. Those changes will be addressed in a later chapter in great detail, and some of the changes I recommend will be appropriate for everyone. Others will be appropriate for only some. But there will be enough suggestions so that *you* can succeed with this plan.

Okay, let's get started with the Three Simple Steps to getting totally out of debt in about five to seven years, including your mortgage.

Step #1: No New Debt

I said these were simple steps, didn't I? Well, that is about as simple as I can get it: *no new debt.* For those of you who may be asking what I mean, let me put that into English for you. "No new debt" in English really means "no new debt." But Bob ... I can hear the screams right now. What about a new car? I'll address that later. In the meantime, no new debt. What about Christmas? I'll address that later. In the meantime, no new debt. What about emergencies? I'll address that later. In the meantime, no new debt. What about getting our first house. Okay, I will give you this. It is probably not feasible for most of you to save up and pay cash for a new house (or a not-so-new one, for that matter). If you are buying your first house, you may need to get a mortgage. Again, we will talk a lot about mortgages later. But did you hear what I said in this paragraph? Other than possibly borrowing for your house, no new debt. Period! No new debt. Say it with me: "No new debt." Say it again: *"No new debt."* One more time (I really want you to get this one down): ***"No new debt."***

See, that was really pretty simple, wasn't it? I told you they were simple steps. (I know you are shaking your head right now thinking I have lost mine, but keep reading. The further you get into the book, the more you are going to realize that *just maybe* it can be done.) If you really don't think you can accomplish this first step, that's okay. It just means that you have made credit a big part of your life and you cannot imagine life without it. Let me ask you this, then. Can you imagine life without any credit payments? That is a lot easier to imagine, so keep that thought in mind.

Before we get to Step Two, you need to take a few moments to prioritize your debts. Prioritizing is simply a matter of writing down your debts in a certain determined order. As I mentioned earlier, knowing where you are can be a real eye-opener if you have not done it before. So, now that you have your debts listed, you want to put them in a certain order so you can determine how you want to focus your attention. There are several possible ways to prioritize your debts, and experts differ as to what is the best way. Let me tell you some of the different ways, and then I will tell you what I recommend.

Probably the way most experts would prioritize debts is to do so by highest interest rate. This method could be the best financially, but it has its drawbacks. The highest interest rate debt might be the largest debt that you have, so it might take years to pay this first debt in full. If this is the case, you will not see any progress for a long time, and that can become discouraging. This is a tough plan, and with no evident results for a while, you might become frustrated and ready to give up. Also, what happens if the interest rate changes? In some cases the interest rate might go down. At this point, do you change the priority in how you are paying your debts? This can get confusing. I want to say something that you may not realize. You do not have an interest rate problem; you have a cash flow problem. Let me say that again: *You do not have an interest rate problem; you have a cash flow problem.*

Another way is to use a formula to determine a *division answer.* By dividing the balance by the monthly payment, you can get a division answer, and then prioritize the debts by the lowest division answer. This process figures out the debt with the lowest balance and the highest payment (resulting in the lowest division answer). This is actually a pretty good way to prioritize debts, and gets the average person out of debt in about the same time as by prioritizing by highest interest rate. However, this can also be time consuming and somewhat confusing. Also, by using this method, the priorities can change along the way.

The third way is what I consider to be the best way, because it is the easiest way and provides the quickest visible results. This method is simply to prioritize your debt by balance, with the lowest balance being the first priority. List your debts, smallest to largest. As this next step unfolds, you will see results faster, which will keep you motivated to stick with it.

As you go through this process, you might choose to prioritize your debts differently, and that's okay. You might choose to make a debt to your parents the first debt you pay off. Or you might decide to make that old IRS bill the first one you get rid of (this is really not a bad idea, as they can become a real nuisance). What really matters is that you get your debts in some sort of pay-off order, and then proceed to the next step.

Step #2: Piggyback

Just what do I mean by piggyback? You know what it is like to give someone a piggyback ride, don't you? You simply put one person on the back of another. That is the principle that we will be talking about in this section.

As you are paying off your debts, eventually one debt will become paid in full. Let's say you were paying $100 per month for that new computer. Eventually, it is paid off, right? Let me pause right here and ask you this: What is the tendency when you pay off that bill and free up $100 per month? That's right, now you say you have freed up $100 a month, so let's go look for a place to spend it. Let's go find something to buy for $100 a month. And typically, you will find something that is *only* $125 a month, which sends you into a little deeper monthly hole. I know that's what you are thinking, because I have done the same thing in the past.

However, I want you to remember Step One: *No new debt.* Do not for even a moment think about buying something for $100 a month, because from this point forward, you are *never* going to use credit again. In fact, why don't you say that with me: "Never use credit!" Say it again: *"Never use credit!"* One more time: ***"Never use credit!"***

Okay, now that we have that settled, and now that we have freed up $100 a month, what are we going to do with that $100 a month? That's right, we are going to piggyback it onto the next debt. Instead of sending $25 per month for that new dishwasher, now we are going to send in the normal monthly payment of $25, along with the $100 that was going to the computer payment. We are going to send in $125 per month now. By doing that, you will now be able to pay off the second debt a lot faster than normal. Eventually, that second debt gets paid off, so now, what do you do with that $125 each month? That's right, you add the $100 from debt #1 and the $25 from debt #2 to the minimum payment you have been paying debt #3 (let's say it's $50 to a credit card). By sending in $175 each month ($100+$25+$50), debt #3 will be paid off quickly.

There is real power in this piggyback process. Dave Ramsey calls this process the "Debt Snowball." Every time a debt is paid off, the snowball picks up more snow and gets bigger and bigger, and he says by the time you get toward the end, what you have is an avalanche. There is tremendous power by piggybacking. Each time one debt is paid off, the ensuing payment gets bigger and has more force to tackle the next. Bigger and faster. Bigger and faster still. This is why this is a critical step in the process. The piggyback process allows you to focus on one debt at a time. Let me tell you about the power of focus. If you walk outside on a bright, sunny day, that sun feels pretty warm, doesn't it? But, what if you walked out into that same sunlight with a magnifying glass and a piece of paper? Talk about some power. That is the power of focus. But, what if that light were focused even more. The result is a laser beam that can cut through steel. Again, that is the power of focus. We want to use the same focus in tackling our debts.

By continuing this process throughout all your debts, the average person will be out of debt in about nine to eleven years, including their mortgage. But wait, I said the average person will be out of debt in about five to seven years, including mortgage. How is this accomplished? The answer is obvious. I have given you two of the three simple steps to get us this far. To get out in a faster time frame, you simply need to go to Step Three.

Step #3: Accelerate

Well, you have now come to the realization that as of *today* you will no longer use credit. You have prioritized your debts and are ready to begin the Piggyback process. However, you have got to get serious about this plan, so we need to add Step Three. When I say accelerate, what do I mean? I am simply telling you that you need to do what every financial planner would tell you to do. Every financial planner would tell you to "Pay Yourself First." They recommend that you pay yourself 10 percent of your monthly income, before you begin paying your bills. Actually, I disagree with that, because, as I mentioned in Chapter Three, we need to give first to the Lord. Okay, you are giving to the Lord and every Christian financial planner would tell you, now you need to "Pay Yourself First" with the next 10 percent. You may have heard the phrase: 10/10/80. That simply is what most Christian financial experts would tell you. Give the Lord the first 10 percent, pay yourself with the next 10 percent, and learn to live on the 80 percent that remains. Well, I can agree somewhat to that; however, I recommend that the second ten percent *not* be put into savings, but rather put toward paying off your debts. To accelerate means that you find an extra 10 percent of your monthly gross income (gross means before taxes) and add those funds to this process. I have had many people tell me, "Bob, my income really is "gross." (I cannot do anything about your income, but if it is gross, then *you* do something about it.)

Let me add two more thoughts. First, if your only debt is your mortgage, I recommend that your accelerator be 20 percent of your income. This should not be a problem, because a person with only a mortgage has no other debts and therefore no other debt payments. Second, the 10 percent (or 20 percent) that I recommend is only a guide. You might not be able to find the whole 10 percent initially, but don't let that stop you. Start where you are. Or, you might be able to find a lot more than 10 percent, and that will only serve to get you out of debt a lot faster and increase the amount you can save monthly for retirement.

How much is that 10 percent? Well, if your gross household income is $36,000 per year, that figures to be $3,000 each month. Ten percent of that would be $300. That's right, your accelerator would be $300 each and every month. If your household income is $60,000 per year, that figures to be $5,000 each month, so your accelerator would be $500 each and every month. If you are fortunate and your annual household income is $120,000, that translates to $10,000 each month, so the 10 percent accelerator would be $1,000 each and every month.

Many of you reading this are saying, "Bob, you have got to be kidding. I do not have the 10 percent of gross income, because I am living paycheck to paycheck right now. I guess this plan will not work." Please, bear with me until Chapter Nine, and I will show you that you *do* have this 10 percent. Those funds *are* in your budget right now; you just have to look closely. Let me say right now, though, that you have got to *want* to find it.

I would like you to *assume* that the funds are there, follow me through the description that follows, and then I will surprise you by showing you where those funds are when we get to the Chapter Nine. Are you with me right now? Are you? Are you ready to begin the process?

Okay, you have determined that you have the extra 10 percent of your gross income to accelerate the debt repayment process. Are you going to take a few dollars and apply to this debt, a little bit over on this one, a chunk on the car, and a few hundred dollars extra principal on the house? No—this is the fastest way to nowhere. We are going to focus, like I said in Step Two. We are going to apply the entire 10 percent to the first priority debt—the smallest debt you have.

Here is how the process works. Month One, you pay the full accelerator plus the normal monthly payment to Debt #1, and you make minimum payments to everything else. Month Two, you pay the full accelerator plus the normal monthly payment to Debt #1, and you make minimum payments to everything else. What are you going to do in Month Three? That's right, you pay the full accelerator plus the normal monthly payment to Debt #1. By the time you get to Month Three (and quite possibly much sooner), you probably paid off Debt #1. Let's say that it did take the full three months. Now what?

For Month Four, you take the full accelerator plus the minimum payment for your smallest debt (Debt #1) and you add that to the minimum payment for your next smallest debt (Debt #2). You continue to do this until Debt #2 is paid off (probably only another three to six months). Now what? That's right! We take all those funds that we were paying monthly to Debt #2 (the accelerator, the minimum payment for Debt #1, and the minimum payment for Debt #2) and we add them to the minimum payment we have been making on Debt #3. So now we pay all this onto Debt #3 and make minimum payments to everything else.

By accelerating, you have now paid off everything—the credit cards, car loans, student loans, personal loans, yes, and even the mortgage—in about five to seven years. I have had people come up to me in the workshops that I teach and say, "Bob it's going to take me eleven years." Well that's okay. Isn't eleven years a lot better than the twenty-eight or twenty-nine years you have left today?

The five to seven years is an average. I have seen many cases where it is actually two or three years. The good news is: debt freedom will happen a lot sooner by using this plan than by using your current plan (if you even have one).

Let's run through a quick exercise to give you a little bit of *hope* right away. I have included a typical American's situation to illustrate this process. Their household income is $54,000 per year (or $4,500 per month).

Debt	Balance	Min. Monthly Payment
Mortgage	$120,000	$850
2nd Mortgage	13,000	410
Visa	3,800	120
Bill's Car	8,500	340
Discover	900	30
MasterCard	1,600	50
Student Loan	7,200	200
TOTAL	$155,000	$2,000

You need to do the same thing. List all of your debts: who do you owe, how much do you owe, and the minimum monthly payment. Remember, a debt is something that can be paid off. A utility bill is not a debt, and neither is rent, because these can never be paid off.

First, total up all your debts. (In our example, total debt is $155,000.)

Second, total up all your minimum monthly payments. (In our example, minimum monthly payments total $2,000.) Third, determine the accelerator and add it to the monthly debt payment amount. Remember, the accelerator is 10 percent of the monthly gross income. (In our example, with a $4,500 monthly gross income, our accelerator of $450 is added to the minimum monthly payment amount of $2,000, giving us an accelerated monthly payment amount of $2,450.)

Now look at Table B.

Come down the left-hand column until you find the number closest to your total debt. (In my example, total debt is $155,000, so I come down to $150,000.) Now circle that number.

Next, going across that line to the right, proceed until you come to the number closest to your accelerated monthly payment. In my example, accelerated monthly payment is $2,450 ($2,000 monthly payment plus $450 accelerator), so I go to the right on the $150,000 line until I come to $2,413. Again, circle that number.

Finally, go directly up that column to find approximately how long it will take to get totally out of debt. (In my example, going up from $2,413, I come to seven years.) Circle that number.

Table B

Debt Elimination Time Calculator

Total Debt	1 Year	2 Years	3 Years	4 Years	5 Years	6 Years	7 years	8 Years	9 Years	10 Years
$1,000	$87	$46	$32	$25	$21	$18	$16	$15	$14	$13
3,000	262	137	95	75	62	54	48	44	41	38
5,000	437	228	159	124	104	90	80	73	68	63
7,000	612	320	223	174	145	126	113	103	95	89
10,000	875	457	318	249	208	180	161	147	135	127
15,000	1,312	685	477	373	311	270	241	220	203	190
20,000	1,749	914	636	498	415	361	322	293	271	253
30,000	2,624	1,371	954	747	623	541	483	440	406	380
40,000	3,498	1,827	1,272	995	830	721	644	586	542	507
50,000	4,373	2,284	1,590	1,244	1,038	901	804	733	677	633
75,000	6,559	3,426	2,385	1,866	1,557	1,352	1,207	1,099	1,016	950
100,000	8,745	4,568	3,180	2,489	2,076	1,803	1,609	1,465	1,354	1,267
125,000	10,931	5,711	3,975	3,111	2,595	2,253	2,011	1,831	1,693	1,583
150,000	13,118	6,853	4,770	3,733	3,114	2,704	2,413	2,198	2,031	1,900
200,000	17,490	9,137	6,360	4,977	4,152	3,605	3,218	2,930	2,709	2,534

Total Debt	1 Year	2 Years	3 Years	4 Years	5 Years	6 Years	7 years	8 Years	9 Years	10 Years
$250,000	21,863	11,421	7,950	6,221	5,190	4,506	4,022	3,663	3,386	3,167
300,000	26,235	13,705	9,540	7,466	6,228	5,408	4,827	4,395	4,063	3,800
350,000	30,608	15,990	11,130	8,710	7,265	6,309	5,631	5,128	4,740	4,343
400,000	34,981	18,274	12,720	9,954	8,303	7,210	6,436	5,860	5,417	5,067
450,000	39,353	20,558	14,310	11,198	9,341	8,111	7,240	6,593	6,094	5,700
500,000	43,726	22,842	15,900	12,443	10,379	9,013	8,045	7,325	6,771	6,334
550,000	48,098	25,127	17,490	13,687	11,417	9,914	8,849	8,058	7,449	6,967
600,000	52,471	27,411	19,080	14,931	12,455	10,814	9,653	8,790	8,126	7,601
650,000	56,843	29,695	20,670	16,175	13,493	11,717	10,458	9,523	8,803	8,234
700,000	61,216	31,979	22,260	17,420	14,531	12,618	11,262	10,255	9,480	8,867
750,000	65,589	34,264	23,850	18,664	15,569	13,519	12,067	10,988	10,157	9,501
800,000	69,961	36,548	25,440	19,908	16,607	14,420	12,871	11,720	10,834	10,134
850,000	74,334	38,832	27,030	21,152	17,645	15,322	13,676	12,453	11,511	10,767
900,000	78,706	41,116	28,620	22,397	18,683	16,223	14,480	13,185	12,189	11,401
950,000	83,079	43,401	30,210	23,641	19,720	17,124	15,285	13,918	12,866	12,034
1,000,000	87,451	45,685	31,800	24,885	20,758	18,026	16,089	14,650	13,543	12,668

Let me recap quickly.

In my example, with $155,000 in debt and an accelerated monthly payment of $2,450 ($2,000 minimum monthly debt payments plus an accelerator of $450), all debt will be eliminated in approximately seven years.

How about you? Is it five years, seven years, three years, nine years? Is your number just barely off the page? If so, please *do not* be discouraged. This simply means that it will take eleven or twelve years, a far cry from the twenty-eight or twenty-nine years that you probably have right now.

This should give you a little bit of *hope* right now. I know you are still saying you do not have that 10% accelerator, but please, bear with me. You should be saying, "*When* I find that 10 percent, then I'll be able to do this." Like I have said all along, we will discuss where to find these funds in the Chapter Nine. However, before we get there, I want you to learn the process, and then I want to give you a big dose of *hope* in a nutshell.

7

The Process

So now, you have the Three Simple Steps to getting totally out of debt in a short period of time:

1) **No new debt:** (remember, in English, that means "no new debt").

2) **Piggyback:** when you get one debt paid off, you take the funds that were going to that debt and add them to the minimum payment for the next debt according to how you prioritized your debts.

3) **Accelerate:** You want *(need)* to find 10 percent of your gross income to accelerate this entire process. (If your only debt is a mortgage, that figure should be 20 percent.) We will talk about where that money is coming from in Chapter Nine, and even though you may be feeling like it isn't there, let me assure you it *is* there. That money is in your current budget—you just have to look at your budget from a different angle.

Now that you have your debts prioritized (I recommend the smallest debt being the first debt), and now that you have found that 10 percent (after you read Chapter Nine), you are now ready to begin the process. I am going to give you the numbers again from Bill and Susie Consumer—typical Americans. As I explain how they would eliminate their debts, you can use the same process to work your plan.

Here are the debts for Bill and Susie Consumer. By the way, as they go through this process, they will be thinking about changing their names, because they will no longer be living like consumers. Their new names will be Bill and Susie Steward. (See Chapter Fifteen). So here is a list of what they owe. Notice that the debts have been prioritized by balance (lowest balance first), regardless of what the interest rate might be.

Debt	Balance	Min. Monthly Payment	Payoff Priority
Discover	$900	$30	1
MasterCard	1,600	50	2
Visa	3,800	120	3
Student Loan	7,200	200	4
Bill's Car	8,500	340	5
2nd Mortgage	13,000	410	6
Mortgage	120,000	850	7
TOTAL	$155,000	$2,000	

Bill earns $36,000/year ($3,000/mo), and Susie earns $18,000/year ($1,500/mo.). Their total annual income is $54,000. Their total monthly income is $4,500. That means that Bill and Susie will have an accelerator of $450 per month (10 percent of their monthly gross income of $4,500.)

Before you look at these numbers and think that this is nowhere close to your situation, remember that I said this is a typical American. In the Denver area where I live, a $120,000 mortgage is rare. If we looked at the average Denverite, I believe that number would be closer to $250,000, and many have mortgages over $400,000. I am sure there are places around the country where the average mortgage is much higher still. I also know that in many parts of the country that number ($120,000) is far above the average, and in many areas, the average mortgage is under $50,000. But I know that the average income in the South Denver area is not $54,000 per household, but rather over $85,000. The same is true around other parts of the country: where the average mortgage is less, so is the average income.

I want to add something right here. Debt increases proportionately to income. As a person's income increases, typically, so does debt. We, as Americans, have a tendency to live on the edge of our income. If income goes up drastically, unfortunately, so does our standard of living. As I shared in Chapter Three, when our income goes up, it should not be our standard of living that increases, but rather our standard of giving. Hopefully, after reading this book, you will want to make that change in your life as well.

We briefly talked about the process in the last chapter, but let's put some numbers to it. I mentioned that we want to take the entire 10 percent accelerator

($450 in this case) and apply it *all* to debt Number One.

Okay, here we go. By adding the $450 accelerator to the minimum monthly payment of $30 for Discover (Debt #1), we have $480 for our accelerated monthly payment to apply to Discover (balance of $900). Here's how the process works. Month One, we would send $480 to Discover, and we would make minimum payments to *all* of the other creditors. That is called *focus.* We are focusing all extra funds on one debt at a time; in this case, it is Discover. Month Two, we send $480 to Discover and we make minimum payments to all the others. By doing this, the Discover will be paid off in just two months. Wow, that was pretty fast, and it is exciting, because in just two months, we went from seven debts to six. This is why we prioritize our debts from smallest balance to largest, because we can begin to see progress right away.

Now that the Discover has been paid off, we have all of a sudden freed up $480 a month. What could we possibly do with that? That's right, we will add that payment to the normal payment for our #2 Debt (MasterCard), which increases the regular monthly payment from $50 to an accelerated monthly payment of $530. So Month Three, what do we do? That's right! We pay $530 to MasterCard and the minimum payments to all the others. We continue doing this every month and three months later (five months total), MasterCard is paid off. Now, we are down to five debts. We are feeling good about the process, because we can see (and feel) the progress.

Now that MasterCard is paid off, we have freed up $530, which we will now add to the minimum monthly payment of our #3 Debt (Visa). That gives us an accelerated monthly payment of $650 that we can use to quickly pay it off. Month Six, we will send $650 to Visa, and continue to make minimum monthly payments to all the other creditors. In just another six months (eleven total), another debt bites the dust.

I am not going to bore you with taking you through the entire process. I think you can see what we have done. But I would like you to notice that it will take two months to pay off Discover, three months for Master Card, six months for Visa, nine months for the student loan, seven months for Bill's car and only eight months for the second mortgage. It has taken thirty-five months (less than three years) to pay off $35,000 of debt, and we have now freed up $1,600 to begin accelerating our mortgage repayment.

Debt	Balance	Min. Monthly Payment	Payoff Priority	Accel. Mo. Pmt.	# of Months
1	2	3	4	5	6
Discover	$900	$30	1	$480	2
MasterCard	1,600	50	2	530	3
Visa	3,800	120	3	650	6
Student Loan	7,200	200	4	850	9
Bill's Car	8,500	340	5	1,190	7
2nd Mortgage	13,000	410	6	1,600	8
Mortgage	120,000	850	7	2,450	49
TOTAL	$155,000	$2,000			84

Month thirty-six, what do we do? That is right! We put the entire $2,450 per month (that is $850 normal payment and $1,600 extra principal) toward paying the house off. At that rate, the house would be paid off in approximately forty-nine more months, or just slightly more than four years. This means the house and everything would be totally paid off in just eighty-four months. That translates into seven years. Seven years, and you are now totally out of debt.

Let me ask you right now, does that number ($2,450) look familiar? That number is the total amount that we applied to debt. We had regular monthly payments of $2,000 and we added $450 as an accelerator. What we have done over the last seven years is that we have paid $2,450 toward debt, whether we had seven debts or only one debt.

At this point, I want to add some fun to the process. I want to say that seven years seems like a long time. You have set your goals to pay off all your debt, but seven years; that's a long time to keep after it. (It's not really, if you are committed and you can see the end results.) What I want to do is break up the seven-year period by throwing in a little bit of celebration along the way. Here is what I suggest. Once you get the Visa paid off (eleven months), I recommend that you consider taking the accelerated payment that was going to Visa ($650 in this case), and celebrate! Take that $650 for one month and do something special with your family. Go on a mini-vacation in the car and spend some time together. Use your imagination. I know $650 won't get you a week-long stay at some fancy hotel, but it will go a long way at several bed and breakfast locations. Check out the historical sites along the way.

Let me ask you. If you take that $650 for one month and do not accelerate your debts, how long does that delay the entire process? That's right! Only one month. I recommend in the process that you find two (maybe three) places along the way where you build in a time of celebration. The reason for this is that seven years is a long time to stay focused. But, if you know that in eleven months you and your family are taking a mini-vacation, that suddenly becomes a short-term goal that everyone can focus on.

I also recommend as you begin this entire process that you get the entire family involved. Let them know what you are doing. Get their input as to where to go and what to do for the times of celebration. Also, let them know that you are changing the way you are spending your money, and things will not be the same as they were. It is *critical* that the entire family becomes involved. If either the husband or the wife is excited about the plan, and the other is not, then the plan will *not* work. It becomes a time of struggle, with one being the free-spender and the other the frugal tightwad. Both must be involved, both must be excited, and both must be committed in order for this plan to work. Also, give the children a chance to contribute to the plan by possibly giving up an expensive activity. Don't think that they definitely will not give something up. Your children might surprise you if you have a plan and that plan has some rewards.

Here are two examples of how you can celebrate. One couple, using the situation above, just before they started accelerating their home mortgage, decided to delay the process for two months, take the $1,250 accelerated payment in their situation for two months ($2,500), and planned to take a ten-day cruise. They knew that would delay the process for two months, but that is what they wanted to do. I can only imagine what they were talking about on that cruise. My guess is they were saying that it wasn't that hard to make it those past three years, but they were excited because now they were going to get the house paid off and be totally debt-free. They would have *no* payments!

Another couple was debt-free, except for the home mortgage, and they were planning on having it paid off in about two years. The family decided that once the house was paid off, they would take a three-week vacation to Disney World. Wow, do you think the children were excited? They were not running to their parents saying, "I have got to get those fancy, high jumping tennis shoes endorsed by the great athlete," or "I have got to get those brand name slacks." No, they were saying, "We just have to get some tennis shoes or some regular slacks, because we have got to get to Disney World."

The key is that you and your spouse must start this plan and you must start it now. It might be a little difficult getting started, but I want you to look ahead. What are the rewards for you? If you are having trouble getting motivated, maybe this will help. Close your eyes and imagine, "If I had no monthly payments except food, clothing, and gasoline, what would that do for me?" The answer simply is: Freedom. Let me state it this way: No Payments = Freedom.

I know you are still asking the question, "Where am I going to find that 10 percent money to accelerate the process?" That is a great question, and again I must ask you to be patient. We have one more chapter before I will answer that question. But, rest assured! You *do* have that money in your budget. I will simply give you ideas of how and where to find it.

Stop reading right now, and fill in your numbers. Let me encourage you with this. It seems that the more debt a person has, the faster he/she will eliminate all the debts, because there is more going toward the whole process than in the case of someone who has just a few debts. (If you do not have many debts, *do not* run out and buy "stuff" just to have more debts. Start today where you are.)

Debt	Balance	Min. Monthly Payment	Payoff Priority	Accel. Mo. Pmt.	# of Months
1	2	3	4	5	6
TOTAL	$	$			

If you have more debts than spaces, simply copy this page and continue.

8

Hope in a Nutshell

In Chapter Six, I talked about the Three Simple Steps to getting out of debt in about five to seven years, including your mortgage. For you it might be only three or four years, but for others it might be eleven or twelve years. But remember, that is still much better than the twenty-eight or twenty-nine years you currently have left on your debts with your plan.

I am confident that I have just given you a glimmer of hope by showing you that, with a real plan, you can get out of debt quickly. At this point people tell me that they can see the light at the end of the tunnel, and it is different from that oncoming train that previously had been bearing down on them. This is the real light, and although it is just a small glimpse of light, it will get bigger and bigger as you proceed through the process.

However, I want to give you more hope right now for what is in store for you down the road. I want to ask you an obvious question, but I want you to stop and think about the day this will happen. (Five to seven years is not that far away. Glance backward and see how quickly the last five to seven years flew by.) Here is what will happen. You have been paying a fixed amount of funds each month toward your debts for the last several years, and now the time has come that you have no more debts. You just paid off your house. After celebrating with a huge mortgage burning party (be sure to invite me), you now realize that next month you will not have to send all those funds in to your creditors or mortgage lender, because you have no debts. The question now becomes, what will you do will all those funds?

Over the past several years, you have been working so hard to get rid of all the debts, and it has been hard work. But now the time has come and you have no debts. You have been paying $1,000 or $2,000 or even $3,000 each month—month after month—for the last several years, and now, without any creditors, you can use those funds each month to begin saving. (I will talk about the importance of building a six-month cash reserve in a later chapter.)

You can look at your situation *today* and know about when that day will come. You can project *today* what amount of funds you will have to invest each month. You can figure out *today* approximately what size nest-egg you will have at your retirement. You can determine for yourself *today* what amount of income this will provide for you in your retirement years. This should give you hope *today.*

Let's take a look at our typical American who is forty years old. Using the worksheet on the next page, you can estimate what you will have available at the date of your retirement. Let's go through this form step by step.

Build *Real* Wealth

With the *same* money you were using to pay debts!

A. Total Accelerated Monthly Payments ______________

B. Current age ______________

C. Number of years to become debt-free ______________

D. Age at which you are debt-free (B+C) ______________

E. Age at which you want to retire ______________

F. Age at which you are debt-free (Same as D) ______________

G. Number of years to save (E–F) ______________

H. Potential Retirement Wealth ______________
(Table C page 94-95—left column—
use the number closest to A;
Across the top—use the number closest to G)

In Chapter Seven, we saw that the typical Americans, Bill and Susie Consumer, will be out of debt in about seven years, and that includes their mortgage. Using this worksheet, we fill in the Total Accelerated Monthly Payment on Line A. This number is the total of your minimum monthly debt payments plus your accelerator. This is the amount of money that is being sent in each and every month to your creditors, whether you have seven creditors or whether everything is paid off except your mortgage. (In my example, Bill and Susie's Total Accelerated Monthly Payment is $2,450.) Please remember this number, as I will refer to it in a few moments.

Line B is the tough one. What is your current age? All you need to do is pull out your driver's license, get a calculator, and figure it out. The question comes up, what if the husband is older than the wife, or vice versa? Whose age do you use in this calculation? The answer depends upon when you are planning to retire. If you plan to retire when your husband turns sixty-five, then use his current age. If you plan to retire when your wife turns fifty-five, then use her current age. (In my example, Bill is currently age forty.)

Line C is the number of years that you determined in Chapter six that it will take to get totally out of debt. Turn back to the chart in section entitled "Table B" if you do not remember. (In my example, Bill and Susie will be debt free in about seven years.)

Line D is simply the result that you get when you add Line B and Line C. This will tell you when you will be totally debt free—including your mortgage. (In my example, Bill is currently age forty; it will take them seven years to get totally out of debt, so Bill and Susie will be totally out of debt by Bill's age forty-seven.) Pretty simple, so far, isn't it?

Line E is the age at which you plan to retire. I have said before that retirement does not have to be age sixty-five. It could be seventy-five for you, or it could be fifty-five. I want to stress again, as you do this, you must be realistic. Don't say you want to retire at age fifty when you are currently forty-seven and have $300,000 of debt. This is *your* plan, so complete it accordingly, but, let me say it again, please be realistic. (In my example, Bill and Susie plan to retire at Bill's age sixty-five.)

Line F is the same as Line D. When will you be totally debt free? (Bill and Susie will still be out of debt at Bill's age forty-seven.)

Line G is the number of years you have to save, once you are totally out of debt. This is simply the difference between Line E and Line F. (Bill and Susie will be totally out of debt at Bill's age forty-seven; they can begin saving from his age forty-seven to his age sixty-five, for a total of eighteen years to save.)

Line H is determined by going to Table C. Turn there now. You want to come down the left-hand column of that table (Monthly Investment Amount) until you find the number that is closest to Line A, Total Accelerated Monthly Payment. (Bill and Susie's monthly amount from Line A was $2,450, so they would use the $2,400 line.) Next, come across the top row and find the number of years closest to the number on Line G. (Bill and Susie's number was eighteen years, so they would go to the closest number, which is 20 years.) Going across the appropriate Monthly Investment Amount column to the right, and coming down the number of years column, where the two intersect is the total amount of funds you might expect to have at your retirement date. (In Bill and Susie's case, the $2,400 Monthly Investment Amount intersects with the 20-year column, resulting in an approximate retirement nest egg of $1,822,485.) This number is based on an expected average rate of return of 10 percent, which of course is *not guaranteed.* A 10 percent return is actually conservative, because many quality mutual funds have averaged over 12 percent per year for seventy plus years.

I want to ask you, is this number higher than you ever expected it to be? I can answer that for you, because I know most people these days are thinking that if only they can get $100,000–$200,000 by retirement, they will be in great shape. In most cases, that is not going to be sufficient income, because the problem today is not that we are dying too soon—the problem is that we are living too long. When I teach this workshop, I have many people tell me that they will be looking at 2.3 million dollars, or 4.5 million dollars. In their wildest imagination, they could never even dream beyond one quarter of one million dollars

($250,000). What about *you?* That number is higher, isn't it?

Some people do not plan until it's too late. They come to the workshop at age fifty-five and ask, "Where were these principles twenty years ago?" Let me say, the principles were there; these folks were either not exposed to the principles, or they were short-sighted and thought they could wait. If this is you, reading this book today, and you are fifty-five or sixty, please, do not lose heart. If it would take you seven years to get out of debt and you are fifty-five now, that means you will be totally out of debt, including your mortgage, at age sixty-two. Is it better that you start now, or wait until age sixty-two to start?

Wherever you are right now, that is the best time to start. Whether you are twenty-five or sixty, put this plan into action *today.* Do not delay. If you are twenty-five years old, and you delay just one month, that could cost you literally tens of thousands of dollars by age sixty-five.

I pray that this chapter has given you something that maybe you have lost, and that is *hope.* Hope that maybe, just maybe, this plan will work for you. Hope that you can become more in control of your finances. Hope that you will not have to live paycheck-to-paycheck for the rest of your life. What I have done in this chapter is to give you Hope in a Nutshell. This is the easy part, writing down what could happen. This is like the huddle in a football game. We have developed the play (the plan). Now comes the hard part and that is executing the plan. As you head into the next chapter, I will give you a lot of ideas about where you can find all that extra money in your budget each month to be able to accelerate this plan. Some of the things I mention will be easy, and others will be a bit more difficult. But keep one thing in mind. I have said this before, but it bears repeating. You have got to *want* to do this plan. It is not just going to happen; you will have to make some changes, but the pain of the small changes will definitely be worth it in the long run.

Take the hope I have given you, keep it close to your heart, and now let's run the play.

Table C

Wealth Building/Financial Freedom Calculator

Monthly Investment Amount	5 Years	10 Years	15 Years	20 Years	25 Years	30 Years
$ 100	$ 7,744	$ 20,484	$ 41,447	$ 75,937	$ 132,683	$ 226,049
200	15,487	40,969	82,894	151,874	265,367	452,098
300	23,231	61,453	124,341	227,811	398,050	678,146
400	30,975	81,938	165,788	303,748	530,733	904,195
500	38,719	102,422	207,235	379,684	663,417	1,130,244
600	46,462	122,907	248,682	455,621	796,100	1,356,293
700	54,206	143,391	290,129	531,558	928,783	1,582,342
800	61,950	163,876	331,576	607,495	1,061,467	1,808,390
900	69,693	184,360	373,023	683,432	1,194,150	2,034,439
1,000	77,437	204,845	414,470	759,369	1,326,833	2,260,488
1,200	92,924	245,814	497,364	911,243	1,592,200	2,712,586
1,400	108,412	286,783	580,258	1,063,116	1,857,567	3,164,683
1,600	123,899	327,752	663,153	1,214,990	2,122,933	3,616,781
1,800	139,387	368,721	746,047	1,366,864	2,388,300	4,068,878
2,000	154,874	409,690	828,941	1,518,738	2,653,667	4,520,976

Monthly Investment Amount	5 Years	10 Years	15 Years	20 Years	25 Years	30 Years
2,200	170,362	450,659	911,835	1,670,611	2,919,033	4,973,073
2,400	185,849	491,628	994,729	1,822,435	3,184,400	5,425,171
2,600	201,336	532,597	1,077,623	1,974,359	3,449,767	5,877,269
2,800	216,824	573,566	1,160,517	2,126,233	3,715,134	6,329,366
3,000	232,311	614,535	1,243,411	2,278,107	3,980,500	6,781,464
3,200	247,799	655,504	1,326,305	2,429,980	4,245,867	7,233,561
3,400	263,286	696,473	1,409,199	2,581,854	4,511,234	7,685,659
3,600	278,773	737,442	1,492,093	2,733,728	4,776,600	8,137,757
3,800	294,261	778,411	1,574,987	2,885,602	5,041,967	8,589,854
4,000	309,748	819,380	1,657,881	3,037,475	5,307,334	9,041,952
4,200	325,236	860,349	1,740,775	3,189,349	5,572,700	9,494,049
4,400	340,723	901,318	1,823,670	3,341,223	5,838,067	9,946,147
4,600	356,211	942,287	1,906,564	3,493,097	6,103,434	10,398,244
4,800	371,698	983,256	1,989,458	3,644,970	6,368,800	10,850,342
5,000	387,185	1,024,225	2,072,352	3,796,844	6,634,167	11,302,440

Example: If you invest $1,000 each month for 25 years, you will have $1,326,833 in total principal—and you will be able to retire at an income of $11,056 *for the rest of your life* without putting another penny in. Based on average 10 percent Return on Investment.

9

Ten Ways to Find That 10 Percent

Well, the wait is over. We are finally to the chapter that you have been waiting for. You say this plan to get out of debt is a good plan, but you do not have that 10 percent accelerator. You say you are currently living paycheck to paycheck and cannot find even five dollars. Like I have said all along, "You *do* have it." Those funds are in your budget, and I am going to show you where. A word of caution is appropriate here. I will share with you many ideas; some will be appropriate for you and some will not. Some will be easy and some will not. Some you will want to do and some you will not. As you try to determine what is best for you, I want to remind you of one thing. Everything I talk about in this book, and in this chapter in particular, is a matter of choice. I have said this before, but I will say it again. I am not going to twist your arm to do any of this. (It would be hard for me to do, so I won't even try.) You have to decide what is best for you and what is not. Then you have to decide which ones you will do and which ones you will not. I may give you ten great ideas, and you might say, I will do eight of them, but I am not going to do these last two. That is quite all right with me. If you choose to do even one of these ideas, then this book will have had an impact in your life.

Let me say this again. You will think I am crazy when I mention a couple of these, because you have never heard of this so far. Does that make my way wrong? You might think I am crazy, because that is contrary to traditional thinking. Again, does that make my way wrong? You might say I am crazy, because all your friends are doing the opposite of what I recommend. I ask you now, are all of your friends financially successful? No, I didn't think so. Let me encourage you to at least try my way before you blindly run out and say "no."

As we begin, I want to say we are trying to find 10 percent of our gross monthly income to set aside. If we are trying to find $450, we should not be looking to find $450 in one place. Let me put it this way. If we are trying to find one dollar, we do not want to look for a dollar. We want to look for a bunch of dimes and nickels, and then every so often find a quarter. That is the easiest and least painful way to accomplish this. We do not want to make major changes; we simply want to make a lot of little changes.

Here are the ideas, in no particular order of importance.

1. Consider increasing your auto and homeowners insurance deductible.

If you are the average American, you have a fairly low deductible on both your automobile insurance and your homeowners insurance, because if something were to happen, you do not have the cash to pay a higher deductible. I am going to suggest that you increase your deductible from where it is now (probably $100 or $250 for both auto and homeowners) to $1,000. By doing so, you can save approximately 30–40 percent of your premium. That is a significant amount of savings, just by taking a little bit of risk.

I can hear the wails and moans now: "Bob, I do not have $1,000 to pay as a deductible in case something happens." My question to you is, "Do you have $250?" The response I get most of the time is, "Well ... no." Here is what I recommend you do to get that money. Go ahead and change your deductible right now to $1,000 and you will begin saving 30–40 percent of your premium. I want you to take that savings and put it aside. I want you to build up your savings until you have your $1,000 for a deductible. That might take ten to twenty months, but you probably will not have a claim in that time frame. After you have done that, then take the 30–40 percent savings and begin accelerating your debts.

I want to add something here. I would *strongly* recommend that you save your entire accelerator (whatever it is—it might be $250 a month or $1,000 per month) to build up that $1,000 in cash. This will be your emergency fund in case something unexpected happens. If you do not have an emergency fund, I can almost assure you, something unexpected *will* happen. By saving the entire accelerator, you can accumulate this $1,000 in one to four months. This will enable you to rest easier.

Let me add one more thought to this item. If you and your entire family are healthy, without frequent trips to the doctors, you might even consider raising your health insurance deductible to $1,000. If you have group insurance, check with the benefits specialist at work. This could save you additional funds each month, which can then be used to increase your accelerator.

2. Buy the right amount of life insurance.

Some people think that the purpose of life insurance is to make the family wealthy. That is just not true. I know people who have so much life insurance that they are insurance-poor. They want to leave a large inheritance to their children. In my mind, that is just plain stupid. Too many people are hurt by receiving large sums of money and no training of how to use it. Let me just say that the purpose of life insurance is to replace the income of the person who is no longer alive to produce an income. In Proverbs, we read, "A good man leaves an inheritance to his children's children." The only way to do that is to leave a proper inheritance to your children *and* the wisdom of how to handle it. That way you will insure the inheritance makes it to the grandchildren. Great wealth should *never* be left to your children. If you have great wealth, leave most of it to your church or other charity. Leave to your children only enough that it will not negatively impact their lifestyle or their way of thinking.

So what is the right amount of life insurance to carry? I recommend that a person have between five and ten times their annual gross income (before taxes) in life insurance. If a person makes $50,000 per year gross income, that person should have between $250,000 and $500,000 in life insurance. That way, if a person were to die prematurely, the spouse and family would have enough to continue living comfortably, although not luxuriously. A better figure between $250,000 and $500,000 can be determined by considering several things: balance of mortgage, amount of other debts, age of spouse and age(s) of children, college aspirations, etc. With the inexpensive cost of insurance (see the next item), I would recommend that a person consider a number closer to the ten times annual income. It is better to have a little too much than not quite enough.

Let's talk about group insurance through work. I have heard too many times that a person has five times annual income in group insurance and therefore does not need any personal life insurance. I disagree with that, because I don't know of anyone who can say for certain that they will still be employed ten, five, two, or even one year down the road. When a person leaves his employer (or his employer leaves him), in most cases the life insurance leaves as well. I also don't know of anyone who can say for certain that they will still be insurable in ten, five, two, or one year later. If at that point a person is looking to get life insurance to replace the group insurance, and he has become un-insurable, he will not be able to get the coverage. His family will then be left with nothing in the event of a premature death. Again, with the inexpensive cost of insurance, I would recommend that a person *not* consider their group insurance at all as meeting a part of the life insurance need.

Here's another question. Does a non-working spouse need life insurance? First, most spouses who stay at home with their children are actually working harder than those with jobs. (I have learned over my many years of counseling not to ask the spouse, "Do you work?", but rather, "Do you work outside the home?") They do work hard; they just do not get a paycheck. Do they need life insurance? Absolutely, they do. I would recommend that they secure at least $150,000 to $250,000 in life insurance, because without that parent, the working parent needs to replace the childcare worker, the cook, the taxi cab driver, the launderer, etc., and all that takes money.

3. Buy the right kind of life insurance.

There are basically two kinds of life insurance, and it is important for someone trying to get out of debt to get the right kind. I want to discuss both kinds and then let you know which kind you should have. This illustration will be extremely simplified, but will very clearly make the point. The first kind of life insurance is what I call *cash value* insurance. You pay the insurance premium and over the years you accumulate cash value. There are many different names for this, including Whole Life, Permanent Life, Ordinary Life, Adjustable Life, Universal Life, Variable Life, Universal Variable Life, and the list goes on. The second kind of life insurance is called *term* insurance. There is no cash value available. Very simply: if you die, the insurance company pays; if you do not die, the insurance company does not pay.

Which is the best kind of insurance? I want to tell you that cash value insurance is the best kind of life insurance—"for the company." Why do you think insurance companies have large buildings? The answer is because they are very profitable. Cash value insurance is a very profitable product for them, and they advertise all the tremendous benefits of the product to the American people, and the people buy it.

Also, cash value insurance is the best kind of insurance—"for the agent." I know, because I used to sell it. There are huge commissions paid to the agent on the sale of cash value insurance. As a Certified Financial Planner (CFP) for nearly twenty-five years, I sold a lot of insurance over the years, and a little bit of it has been cash value insurance. When I was trained by a company, I was instructed that the best kind of insurance was always cash value insurance, because with term insurance a person is simply *renting* the insurance. With cash value insurance, a person now owned something. I was constantly trained about the benefits of the newest kind of cash value insurance. Never, and I mean *never,* was I trained about the benefits of term insurance. Why not? Because the benefits to the company were minimized and the commissions to the agent were also minimized. Most life insurance agents starting out needing to make some good money quickly so they can remain in the business and cash value insurance provides that. The agents are indoctrinated with only one side of the story—the side that benefits the company. The agent figures it's the best for the client, because the company tells him it is best for the client.

I want to be very clear when I say this. For 99+ percent of the people reading this book, there is only one kind of life insurance you should consider, and that is term life insurance. More specifically, I recommend fifteen-year or twenty-year guaranteed level term insurance. Let me explain what exactly that is. The life insurance company guarantees that the face amount of the policy (let's say $350,000) will remain level for the term (let's say twenty years). They also guarantee that the premium (let's say forty dollars per month) will remain level for the twenty years. However, in year twenty-one, the premium will jump, possibly to $400 per month. I can already hear the life insurance agents saying, "You can't afford that, so you should be buying cash value insurance now for $100 per month." Let me explain further what I recommend.

If you want to get out of debt, let's assume that it doesn't take five to seven years (including the mortgage), but let's say it takes ten years. After the ten years, you now have $2,000 or $3,000 each month that used to go toward debt payments (mortgage, credit cards, car loans, student loans) that you can begin saving. If you were to save $2,000 per month for the next ten years, at 10 percent you would have $409,690. Let me ask you now. Why do you need that $350,000 life insurance policy, when you have over $400,000 in your mutual fund? The answer is simply: "You don't." You have now become self-insured, which means that if you suffer a premature death, your family will be just fine (financially) because your income will be replaced by drawing income from the $400,000.

Additionally, I recommend that every three to four years you check the price of this guaranteed level term insurance. There is a lot of competition in the life insurance industry, and there is a good chance that you can get another fifteen- or twenty-year policy at a cost less than the first one, even though you are now three to four years older. By doing this, you will extend that fifteen- or twenty-year period. Does this mean that you *must* keep this insurance in force for the full term? Absolutely not! You might be in a position where you want to cancel the policy after twelve years, because you have accumulated sufficient funds in your mutual fund. All you need to do is to stop paying the premium, and the insurance will no longer be in force. Now you can save that additional forty dollars per month.

You might be wondering, should I cancel this cash value policy, even though I have had it for five or ten or fifteen years? Yes and No! *No,* you do not want to cancel your cash value insurance if you are no longer insurable. Also, *no,* you do not want to cancel this policy until you have term life insurance in place, because you don't want to be five minutes without life insurance. And *yes,* once your term insurance is in place, you should cancel this policy, even if you have had it a long time. I have *never* seen a case where it is better to keep the policy instead of changing to term insurance and using the rest to pay off your debts and then save. You should take whatever cash value you have and pay off some debts right now. (Be sure to establish your $1,000 emergency fund if you do not already have it.)

Not only is term insurance less expensive because it builds no cash value, but it is significantly less expensive. It is not uncommon for a person to get three to four times the face amount of insurance for about one-forth of the cost. It frustrates me when I see a person with a $100,000 cash value policy and nothing else. The reason is that the agent sold them a high commission policy, and that was all he could sell within the client's budget. This is a huge disservice to the client who probably needed $300,000 to $400,000, and could get a term policy for the same or less money each month.

I would be remiss if I did not mention that your agent is not incompetent because he or she sold you cash value insurance. There are many fine people who sell life insurance, and some have been doing it for years. It is just that they are ignorant to the way cash value insurance really works, because they have been fed propaganda from the company for many years. Like I mentioned, I used to sell the stuff (I call it *trash value* insurance), but then one day I got a brain. I saw the light as to how money really works, and trash value insurance is very clearly *not* in your best interest. Get rid of it! (By the way, it took me several months to come to this conclusion because I had been duped by the insurance companies as well. After I took a *long "open-minded" look,* the results were very clear—it was trash-value insurance.)

Many years ago a gentleman by the name of A.L. Williams started a company named (of all things) A.L.

Williams. His strategy was this: Buy term and invest the rest. He suggested a person get term insurance, then get rid of the cash value insurance, and take the savings (fifty dollars per month or one hundred dollars per month or whatever it was) and invest it into mutual funds. I want to tell you right now. In my opinion, A.L. Williams was *almost* right. He said buy term and invest the rest. I say, "Buy term, use the difference to accelerate your debt elimination, and then (and only then) invest the rest. We will talk more about savings later in this chapter.

4. Eliminate P.M.I. (Private Mortgage Insurance).

Let me explain just what Private Mortgage Insurance is. P.M.I. is insurance that does absolutely nothing for you, the homeowner. It is acquired by the lending company (but you pay the premiums) and it provides security for the lender. In the event you do not make your monthly payments and you are evicted from the house, the lender will sell the house. If the selling price is less than the mortgage balance, the insurance company will pay the difference to the lender. This way, the lender is not at risk of loss. In many areas of the country, however, houses appreciate, and the chances of a lender losing money are small, but yet the P.M.I. is put in place anyway.

A general rule is that if you have been in your home for at least two years and you have at least 20 percent equity in your home, there is a good chance that you can eliminate the P.M.I. You must contact the lender to see if this is appropriate. If you can drop the coverage, this will free up between $50 and $300 each and every month.

5. Do not loan money at a 0 percent interest rate.

You might be wondering what I am talking about, so I will explain. Let me ask you this. Would you like to borrow money at 0 percent interest? Your first thought is an obvious "Yes." But, remember what I said earlier: *Never use credit,* not even at a zero percent interest rate. I will talk more about that later. But if I were to ask you if you wanted to loan money at 0 percent interest, you would surely say, "No way." Well, every year I see it over and over again. I see broke people getting large tax refunds. I see $3,000 to $6,000 tax refunds all the time. Let's assume you got a $3,600 tax refund. I want to translate into English what has just happened the past year. Every month, you have loaned Uncle Sam $300, and at the end of the year, those funds ($3,600) are sent back to you, with 0 percent interest!

I hear people trying to justify a big tax refund by saying things like, "Oh, I use the refund to pay off my debts." Let me just say—that is *stupid.* Why don't you build a little discipline into your life, take the $300 each month, and accelerate paying off your debts monthly. Not only will you not be loaning your money at 0 percent interest, you will actually be saving 18 percent interest (or whatever the interest rate is) on the debt you are accelerating. Do you remember what Ben Franklin said years ago? "A penny saved is a penny earned." You have just earned that 18 percent on that money each month, because you have not had to pay it.

I also hear people say, "Oh, I use the refund for my vacation fund." Let me say it again. You must build some discipline into your life, and take that $300 every month and put it into the bank, and then you can actually earn some interest. In Matthew 25:27, Jesus said to the unwise steward that he should not have buried the money in the ground, but that he should have at least put the money in the bank and earned interest. If you consistently, year after year, keep getting large tax refunds, I believe you are acting as an unwise steward. If you are looking for extra funds to accelerate your debt elimination plan, then a large tax refund should not be for you.

So, how do you stop getting a big tax refund? You will need to contact your CPA, tax preparer, or the human resources person at work. Tell them you want to increase your withholding allowances so you have less held out each payday from your check. If you talk with your CPA or tax-preparer, he or she will be able to help you determine the changes that need to be made. You might be instructed to change your withholding allowances to seven. Your first thought is that you and your spouse do not have five children, so how could you claim seven. The withholding allowances you claim are not determined by how many dependents you have, but they are used to help you make sure you have the proper amount of taxes withheld.

If you do not have a CPA or tax-preparer, I have included a form below to help you determine the proper amount to be withheld. You will also need IRS Publication 15-T to determine what number of withholding allowances will enable you to have the proper amount withheld. (Go to www.irs.gov, search for "forms and publications," and then find Publication 15-T. Then find the proper pay frequency for you: monthly, semi-monthly, bi-weekly, or weekly.) This is the form you can use in the middle of the tax year. You will notice on line K a safety buffer of $500. If you cut things too close and miss by $200 or $300, you will still get a small refund. I would rather you get a few hundred dollars back than have to pay in a few hundred dollars. Once you make that change, you are set for the balance of this current tax year. I would *strongly recommend* that you re-calculate the amount at the beginning of the next tax year as well to make sure the proper amount is still being withheld.

Many people, in their search for the 10 percent accelerator, find the bulk of the money in this one category. I hope the same is true for you. If not, do not be discouraged. Just keep reading, because there are still several additional ways that you can use.

Tax Projection for Year 20____

A. Income (year to date)

Husband ______________

Wife ______________

Total income (year to date) ______________

B. Projected income (balance of year)

Husband(# of checks times ________) ______________

Wife (# of checks times ________) ______________

Total projected income ______________

C. Total projected income for the year (A+B) ______________

D. Exemption allowance (# in family times current amount allowed) ______________

E. Subtotal (C–D) ______________

F. Projected itemized deductions ______________

G. Taxable income (E–F) ______________

H. Tax (from tax table) ______________

I. Withheld so far

Husband ______________

Wife ______________

Total withheld so far ______________

J. Still needed to be withheld (H – I) ______________

K. Safety buffer + 500

L. Total amount still needed ______________

M. Number of checks remaining this year ______________

N. Amount needed from each check (L/M) ______________

O. Number of withholding allowances to be claimed ______________

(See IRS Publication 15-T)

6. Save money at the grocery store.

It is amazing how much money we can spend at the grocery store. After our mortgage payment and car payment, our next largest expense is usually at the grocery store. There are entire books devoted to saving money on food, but I will give you what I consider to be *five quick tips* on how most of you can save a lot of money each month, without a lot of change. Some people, by making some of these changes, can save up to $50 a month. I have seen many, really wanting to get out of debt, saving over $200 a month in this category alone. Remember, these are just ideas that might work for you. You decide how and how much you want to change to get yourself out of debt.

Tip #1: When you go to the store, always *take a list* with you. Have you ever gone to the store for just three items and walk out with three bags of groceries. You do not need to answer that one—I know you have. We all have. However, if you take a list with the specific items, and have a desire to stick to it, you will be surprised that you will buy just what is on the list. When I run to the store, and if I have six items on the list, I will mention to the checker, "Hey, I have six items on my list, and I only bought six things." The checker will get this funny look on her face and mumble something like, "Nobody ever does that."

Let me tell you what happens if you go without a list. Let's say you are having that casserole tonight and one of the items you need is cream of mushroom soup. At the store, you think, gosh, I need to buy some soup, because we do not have any at home.

So, you buy two cans, and you get home only to discover that you already had six cans in the pantry. Or, you think, I have some at home already, so I don't need to buy any more, and you get home only to discover that you do not have any. This means another trip to the store to get one item (and if you go without a list, that means one full grocery bag, right?).

Here is a startling statistic: Do you know that at any given moment, 60 percent of the people in grocery stores are buying *today's* meal? Talk about a lack of planning. Talk about a lot of trips to the store each month. Talk about a lot of time spent. Talk about a lot of gas wasted. Simply make a list and stick to it.

Tip #2: *Use smart coupons.* Smart coupons are those you use to buy something you had intended to buy anyway. Dumb coupons, as I call them, are those that you use to buy the national brand, and even when doubled, you still pay more than the local store brand. I want to tell you what happens at the food plant. At the Kuner's plant, they are packing green beans every day. One day the foreman says, "Stop the presses, today is Wednesday, put on the Albertson's label." That's right, they are the same green beans, but you say, "I want to buy the 'national' brand, not the local brand." This is true for most canned goods. Dumb coupons are also those used to buy things we do not need. I have heard people say, "This is a great deal with the coupon." When asked if they needed the item they reply, "Well, no, but it's too good a deal to pass up." There are coupons that can lower your total food bill, and there are some that can actually increase the total. Use smart coupons.

Tip #3: When you go to the grocery store, *leave your children at home.* Yes, you heard me right. Before I give you the reasons why, let me answer that question from the single parent who says they cannot leave the children home alone. For you single parents, you must find another single parent, ask her to watch your children while you shop, and then you can watch her children while she shops. You must leave your children at home if you want to be successful at the grocery store.

The reason to leave the children at home is simple. Taking them with you to the store encourages all kinds of negative behavior. "Can we get this cereal?" No! "Can I have this candy bar?" No!! The child asks ten times throughout the store if he can get something (something that is not on your list) and eight times you say, No!!! That means that two times you say *yes,* which adds to your food total. If your children are walking, most will tend to wander away from the cart, bringing commands of "get over here right now!" This now adds to your stress level, and the whole process takes longer, which means you have also spent more time. So, very simply save time, money, and stress and leave the children at home.

Tip #4: Here is another good tip. When you go to the store, *leave your spouse at home.* What? That is our time together. Well, if that is the case, you had better look for other time together. In nearly every family there is a spender and a saver—one who loves to buy what pleases the eye and one who is a bit more frugal. Isn't that true in your family? Again, you can save not only money, but time also by shopping without your spouse. I have a friend in Texas who spends $250 per month at the grocery store for a family of four, and the family eats well. You might wonder how she does it. She told me, "it's my husband's job to bring the money in, and it is my job to see that as little as possible goes out." When she gets ready to go to the store, she says, "Honey, will you watch the children for a while? I am going to work." She approaches grocery shopping as a job and she has become very good at it. Just think, if you could only spend two hundred fifty dollars per month at the grocery store, how much would that free up in your budget to use to accelerate your debts? What if you only saved half that amount? In order to be good at shopping, you must leave your children AND your spouse at home.

Tip #5: Here is the last tip. *Be sure to separate your impulse items.* When you go to the grocery store with your list, if you pick up anything that is not on your list, that is an impulse item, so you must simply put that item in the child seat. (Remember, there is no child there, because the kiddos were left at home.)

While you are shopping you might pick up ten items that are not on your list. These ten items then will be placed in the child seat. When you get to the checkstand, take a good hard look at those items, and then ask yourself this question. "How important are these items, compared to my goal of getting out of debt?" If you have ten items, you might put back eight and keep two (in my case one of those keepers is the chocolate ice cream). Every time you put back one item, it is less money out of your pocket, which translates into more money into your pocket for the accelerator.

Like I mentioned, there are many books with many more tips on how to save money at the grocery store. These are simply a few of the ones I see that people can actually do without having to make a lot of changes.

7. Cut down on conveniences—do things yourself.

A convenience is something that we pay someone else to do, because we don't know how to do it, or we simply don't want to do it our self. Let me give you a few examples: Do you prepare your own income tax? Over 95% of Americans should be able to prepare their own taxes. But they think it is so complicated and they are so fearful of the IRS that they would rather pay the local tax-preparing franchise $200–300 for something that they could learn once with a twenty-five dollar book and a few hours of reading. You might pay a CPA from your church $25 to help you learn how to prepare your own taxes. If the CPA is a friend, you might be able to save even that $25.

Do you pay for someone to mow your lawn or shovel snow from your driveway? I know people with teenage boys who pay up to $35 a week for a lawn service to come in and manicure their lawn. A week later that manicure has lost its pizzazz, so they pay another $35. Wow, that's $140 per month. I also know people with no teenage sons, but with teenage daughters who mow the lawn, and it looks great (and they have saved $140 per month).

Here is another way to cut down on conveniences. I know people come home late and say, "Gee, I don't want to cook and then do dishes. Let's do fast food." Others say, "Gosh, I don't want to fix a brown bag lunch; I want to eat lunch out with my co-workers." Let me share a startling statistic. Do you know the average American worker in the United States spends between $80 and $120 a month eating lunch out? Figure it out. That's only $4 to $6 a day. Let me go one step further. I know people who spend between $80 and $120 a month at the local coffee bar getting a cappuccino and muffin. Now am I saying to totally stop fast food or eating lunch out or the coffee bar? No, I am not. What I am saying is, if you are eating lunch out every day, why not brown bag it two days a week (and still eat lunch out three days a week). By doing this, you could save $30 to $50 a month.

Remember, we are not looking to make major changes, but rather a lot of little changes. Here's a thought! Take your brown bag lunch and go out with the co-workers and sit with them while they eat. Let them know you are trading eating out two days a week for that freedom that will result with having no debts.

Here is one more example. I want to say that I am not very mechanical. (You can verify that with my wife.) However, one thing I do is I change the oil in my car. Instead of paying $25 or $30 to have the oil changed, I do it for less than $10 for the oil and filter. That means I save $15–20 each time I change oil. How many times do you have your oil changed? How many vehicles do you have? Figure it out. The savings could be significant.

There are so many ways that you are spending your money to have something done for you that you could do yourself. Find out what that is, start doing it yourself, and then take that extra money and work that debt elimination plan.

8. Consider refinancing your home.

Over the last 3–4 years, many people have refinanced their home to take advantage of record level low interest rates. With rates continually going down, I would recommend that a person refinance at a *no cost* basis. This simply means there are no costs to do the refinance. Many places were saying they would do a no-cost loan, but what they meant was no out-of-pocket costs. Several thousand dollars of closing costs were then rolled into the new loan. A no cost loan is just that. There are no origination fees or points and no costs for appraisals, credit checks or other fees. A true no cost loan works because the borrower would pay about 1/4% higher than the going rate, and the lender, knowing they were getting a little higher return on their money, would then pay the closing costs and all commissions. With rates currently creeping back, a no cost loan may or may not be the best for you.

The way to determine whether to refinance at all is done simply by comparing how much closing costs you will pay, how much lower the monthly payment will be, and how long it would take you to recover those costs. If you can save $100 per month on your payment to refinance, but it would cost you $3,000 in closing costs, it would then take you 30 months ($3,000 divided by $100 per month) to recover those costs. If you plan to stay in your home for at least another two and one-half years (30 months), then you should do it. You might say it's only $100 a month, and it's not worth it to go through the hassle. Let me assure you, that $100 can sure add to the bottom line as to when you will be out of debt and to how much you will accumulate by retirement.

9. Plan your gift giving throughout the year.

Buying gifts can be a huge expense in your budget. Too many times we are "expected" to give large gifts for anniversaries, birthdays, graduations, weddings, and yes, especially for Christmas. There seems to be an unwritten mandate in some families that says, you "must" give. As we continue looking for ways to find extra money in our budget to use in our debt elimination plan, we must look at the area of gifts. Most of the time, gift-giving is something that can be planned. We can look at the calendar and see how many birthdays we will celebrate, how many anniversaries and graduations we need to plan for. We know Valentine's Day, Mother's Day and Father's Day will come sometime this year. I know sometimes an event comes up that we didn't plan for, like a wedding with a short engagement. But, for the most part, we can plan what we need to do throughout the year. I cannot tell you the number of times I have heard someone say in late November or early December, "Oh my gosh, Christmas is coming. What are we going to do?" Let me ask a foolish question here. As the year progresses through summer and into fall, do you think that December 25th will be on the calendar this year? Like I said, it's a foolish question, but for many, Christmas coming is a surprise. Folks, we know it's coming, so let's plan for it. What normally happens is we didn't plan, so we use our backup plan, which is pulling out the credit card. *Wait,* we cannot do that this year, because we are trying to get out of debt and have decided to *never use credit again.* I did a workshop a few years back (I think it was late November) and one man raised his hand and sheepishly admitted, "Last month (October) I finally paid off last Christmas." Unfortunately, I see that happening too often.

You should have a budgeted amount for gifts that you address every month. To determine that amount, figure out what you plan to spend the entire year—birthdays, anniversaries, Valentine's Day, Mother's Day, Father's Day, Christmas, and whatever else might be on your calendar—and total it up. If that figure comes to $2,400 for the year (I know that sounds like a large number to some of you, but it's reality to many of you), this means one of two things. First, you must save $200 each and every month for gifts, or second, it means you must reduce this $2,400 figure. There is *no* third option.

Here are a few ideas of how you might reduce this figure. First, if you are in a large family with many brothers, sisters, cousins, aunts, uncles, etc., you might consider drawing names for Christmas and buy for just one person in the extended family. Buying one "nice" gift would be a whole lot cheaper and more appreciated than buying a lot of little gifts that in most cases would never be used or worn. Second, keep an eye open for sales throughout the year. My son does a great job of buying gifts for family members. As I write this, I would almost guarantee he has already bought my Christmas gift, even though Christmas is still several months away. This will actually take some thought, but it can save you tremendously. Third, consider making gifts. This used to be the normal way to give gifts, by using skills and talents to give a gift from the heart. Family pictures in a hand-made frame will mean more than that "thing" that will sit on the shelf or be tucked away in the basement. However, we don't have time anymore to spend making gifts; it's just too easy to run down to the mall and pick something up. The best gift we can give is that of our time. By making something, the gift is usually something the person can better use and will appreciate more, because we have given of ourselves and our time. Also, you save money.

10. Minimize retirement plans.

I know you are going to think I have lost it when I tell you this one, but please keep reading, give it a try, and run the numbers for yourself. Remember, we are trying to find at least 10% of our monthly gross income. This one step alone will allow some of you to find the entire 10%. Still others will do this alone and now have 5% for an accelerator. Let me say this again, in case you missed it. *Minimize your retirement plan contributions.* If you are currently contributing to a 401(k), a 403(b), an IRA, or some other retirement plan, I simply say *stop.* Do not contribute any more until you are out of debt. I am *not* saying to pull the funds out. Just stop putting more money in. If you pull your money out, you will be 1) taxed by the I.R.S. (that would be 15% to 28% for most of you), 2) penalized by the I.R.S. (that would be a flat 10% early withdrawal penalty if you are under age 59 1/2), and 3) taxed by your state (In Colorado, that would be a 4.5% tax). That means you would lose between 30% and 43% immediately to taxes and penalties. Don't do that, but *do* stop putting money in. I can hear the objections now, "But Bob, I only have so long to save, I need to start now."

Here's another one I hear all the time. "Bob, I am getting a 25% match from my employer. For every dollar that I put in, my employer matches it with a quarter." I say stop contributing *now.* Then I hear, "Bob, I am getting a 50% match; I am putting in a dollar, and my employer is putting in fifty cents." Stop contributing now. But that's free money. You are right, but I want you to get out of debt before you start saving, so let me say it one more time. Stop contributing *now.* Only once in a while do I hear this. "Bob, I am getting a one-to-one match on the first three percent of my salary. I put in one dollar and they match it with one dollar." Let me make this very clear—take it! However, do not contribute 15% and let them match you on the first 3%. If they match you one-to-one on the first 3%, drop your contribution to 3% to get their match. If you were putting in 15% and getting a 3% match (that's a total of 18% of your salary), I recommend that you drop to 3%, get their 3% (that's a total of 6%), and now you have freed up 12%. There is your entire 10% accelerator plus 2%. I will address *why* we stop retirement savings in the next chapter. Keep reading and you just might agree with me.

Now that we have found the 10% accelerator, I want to give you three suggestions how you can get this entire process working faster still. I call it three ways to *accelerate the accelerator.* These three ways will help you get some immediate cash in your hand to immediately (or very quickly) pay off two or three of your smaller debts.

First, you can *have a garage sale.* I know you, like me and like everyone else, have a lot of stuff in your garage and basement and attic. Go through your entire house and find those objects that you never or rarely use. They are taking up space and providing you with no benefit. Pull them out for a garage sale and price them appropriately. What I mean by this is, do not price it based upon what you think it might be worth, but rather what you would be willing to pay for it if you went to a garage sale. Listen up! *I have a guaranteed way for you to make one thousand dollars at a garage sale.* Are you ready for this? Simply sell 2,000 items for 50 cents apiece. I am *not* kidding. You do have a ton of little things scattered around that you could sell for a half-dollar, and those start adding up. If you did not sell too much this week, have another garage sale next week and mark everything down 50% more. Remember, one man's trash is another man's treasure. Get rid of it if you are not using it and pay toward those debts.

Second, if you have a large savings account, you could *apply funds from these long-term savings* and pay off one or more of your smaller debts. Now be careful, I did not say to pull money from your 401(k), 403(b), or IRA or "qualified" accounts. If you do, you will be taxed and penalized heavily, as we discussed before. But if you received an inheritance and those funds are sitting in your savings account or mutual fund, put them to work for you by accelerating your debt elimination plan. Be sure to hold out $1,000 for an emergency fund.

Third, you might *consider getting a short-term part-time job.* Now I do not mean for the next two or three years, but maybe for the next two or three months. If you live in a large city, you can deliver pizza three-four nights a week and earn an extra $1,000 per month. You can deliver newspapers and earn $750–1,000 per month. These extra funds should be used to knock out a few of your smaller debts and get the whole process going faster.

You can choose to do one, or two, or all three of these. Maybe you can think of other ways to get things rolling faster. This is your plan, and how you respond will reflect just how committed you really are. Remember, when those debts are paid off, the funds that were being used monthly still stays in the mix to eliminate all the other debts faster.

Okay, I have given you a lot of ideas of where the money is to get out of debt faster. You might say, "Bob, I don't want to quit saving now," or "I don't want to change my own oil", or "I don't want to stop eating lunch out." My response to you is: *That's okay.* This is your plan and *you* make the choices that are best for you. But I want you to be brutally honest with yourself. Ask yourself this question: "How important is it for me to get out of debt?" Then make whatever choices you feel are best for you.

When I suggest you find 10% to accelerate your debts, this is merely a guideline. Some may be able to find 15% or 20%. Others may only be able to find 5% (although if you *really* want to get out of debt, I am confident you can find the entire 10%). If you can only find 5% now, start at 5%, but keep looking for ways to increase this. Get up to 10%, but just like we talked about Giving in Chapter Three, when you get to 10%, don't stop there!

10

Should I Really Stop Saving Now?

In the last chapter, I gave you "Ten Ways to Find that Ten Percent." We looked at ten ways to find extra funds to begin accelerating your debt elimination plan. Some of the ways were common sense ideas, like shopping smartly at the grocery store and cutting down on conveniences. These are ideas that you have probably heard many times before. However, I gave you several that I know were totally foreign to you. In fact, you are probably scratching your head right now asking, "Did he really say that?" Yes, I really said that you should not get a large tax refund every year. Yes, I said that you should get rid of that "trash value" life insurance. Yes, I said you should increase the deductibles on your auto and homeowners insurance. And, in answer to the statement you have "never" heard before, let me say this: Yes, I said you should stop saving for retirement now. Stop until you have all your credit cards paid off. Stop until your student loans and cars are paid off. Stop until your mortgage is paid off. *What!* That just doesn't make sense.

As I go through this chapter, I want to convince you to *stop* contributing to your 401(k), your 403(b), your I.R.A., and any long-term retirement savings you might be doing. As much as you might be struggling with this concept, you will see that it not only makes sense, it makes cents and it makes dollars. But, like I have often said before, the good news is, "you" decide what is best for you, and then you can do it. But please, do not just blindly say that this will not work without reading through the chapter. Give this one a fair shot. Then, if you decide you do not want to put this one into the mix, that's okay.

Let's take a look at the form on the next page. There are two different scenarios to consider. In either case, I am making the assumption that Bill and Susie Consumer have found an extra $450 to save for something. On the left side, the first thing Bill and Susie are going to do is to save for a 6-month cash reserve. All the financial experts say you need to build that first. With a gross household income of $54,000 per year ($4,500 per month gross or about $3,400 net), Bill and Susie would need a 6-month cash reserve of about $20,400. By saving $450 per month, it would take them 45 months—that's nearly four years—to save this $20,400. After they did this, they would save that $450 per month in their mutual fund (averaging let's say 10%). At the end of ten years from the start, they would have accumulated $46,624.

What is best for you?

Monthly income is $4,500 gross ($3,400 net)—10% ($450) available to use

Plan A			**Plan B**	
(Conventional wisdom)		or	*(A new idea)*	
(save $450 per month now)			(Use $450/mo. to accelerate debt repayment and then save $2,450/mo.)	
What to do	**months**		**What to do**	**months**
Accumulate a 6-month cash reserve of $20,400 (6 x $3,400) by saving $450/mo.	45		Accumulate a $1,000 emergency fund by saving $450/mo.	3
			Eliminate debt of $155,000	84
			Accumulate a 6-month cash reserve of $6,000 (6 x $1,000) by saving $2,450/mo.	3
Save $2,450/mo. for 6+ years @ 10%	75		Save $2,450/mo. for 30 months @ 10%	30
Total # of months	120		Total # of months	120
After 10 years	$46,624		After 10 years	$83,112
			Difference	$36,488
After 28 years	$550,218		After 28 years	$1,970,445

The choice is yours!

Now, let's suppose instead they chose to take that $450 and put it toward paying off their debts. (For the first 2 1/2 months, they saved their $1,000 emergency fund.) It would take them about seven years to pay off all their debts, even the mortgage. Now they can begin to save their 6-month cash reserve fund. Before they start saving, they need to figure out how much they really need in this fund. They will *not* need $20,400, or $3,400 a month, because, for the last six-plus years, they have learned to live without $2,450 ($2,000 toward debts and $450 accelerator). Therefore, they would only need $1,000 for six months, or $6,000. At $2,450 per month, that six-month cash reserve would be saved in just three months. At this time, now they can begin saving $2,450 each month in their mutual fund. By the end of the same ten-year period, they would have accumulated $83,112 in their mutual fund.

Let me ask you now, what is the difference between the first scenario on the left (saving a six-month cash reserve fund and then saving for retirement) and the second scenario on the right (paying off debt, then saving a six-month cash reserve fund, and then saving for retirement)? By the difference, I do not mean $36,488 ($83,112–$46,624). The real difference is that on the right side, there are no longer any debts. There are no longer any monthly payments. There has been a change in thinking about money. There has been a paradigm shift. On the left, they have continued to pay off old debt, and then incur new debt. Pay off old debt, and then incur new debt. Pay off old debt, and then incur new debt. The truth is, at the end of the ten years, they would probably be worse off, debt-wise, than they are right now, because there has been no change in behavior. Buy that "stuff" now with money they don't have. (Are you worse off debt-wise today than you were ten years ago? Most people answer "yes".)

Now, if we continue this process until the house would be paid off (that would be about 28 years from today), they would have accumulated $550,218 in the first scenario and $1,970,445 in the second. Here is the question you need to ask: Which would you rather have? $550,218 or $1,970,455? This is not a trick question!

Let me ask you. Have I convinced you now to stop investing in your 401(k) or your 403(b)? Have I? You say that you are not yet convinced? That's okay! Most people at this point still are not convinced. Let me just say that if you continue for the next couple pages, I can almost assure you that you will want to stop retirement savings immediately. *(WARNING: Don't read the next several pages unless you have an open mind.)*

I hear people say all the time, "If I stop putting money into my 401(k) plan, that will increase my taxes." Let me just say, I agree that your taxes will increase a little bit. But I will come back to that after this example.

I want to share with you an actual situation that occurred during counseling. A 43-year old gentleman came into our office and he had total debt of

$175,000, which included his mortgage. He had just gone to his financial advisor, who told him what most financial advisors tell people. He found out that at age 62, his 401(k) plus Social Security would provide him an income of $3,100 per month. At first glance, this sounds pretty good, because that's over $37,000 per year. But, and I want to make sure you hear this, *that is only one-half of the story.* His monthly income of $3,100 would be nice, except when you consider that he would have debt payments (house, car, and credit cards) of $2,400 each month. This would give him $700 ($3,100 income less $2,400 for debt payments) each month to live on. Just $700 per month! *This* is the entire story. After working all his life, he would have $700 per month to live on.

When he came into the office, we told him we would get him out of debt in 5–7 years, including the mortgage, but he would have to stop putting money into his 401(k) program. Well, because of his particular situation, it would actually take 10 years to get totally out of debt, so now he would be 53 years old. He would then be able to save the $2,400 each month that was going to debt payments into a good quality mutual fund for a period of 9 years (from age 53 to age 62). At age 62, here is what he would have. His 401(k) and Social Security would not provide $3,100 each month, because he would have stopped putting money in at age 43. However, it would provide an income of $2,000 each month. Additionally, since he had been putting $2,400 each month into a good quality mutual fund for nine years, he has built up a fund of $417,728 (at an assumed rate of 10%). This fund would then provide "lifetime" income of nearly $42,000 per year or $3,500 per month. So, total income at age 62 would then be $2,000 from 401(k) and Social Security, plus $3,500 from his investments, for a total income of $5,500 per month. That is compared to $3,100 per month in the first example.

However, at age 62, his total debt payments, (house, car, and credit cards) would be *zero.* His total income to live on would then be $5,500 per month, compared to $700 in the first example. Here is the question you need to ask yourself. Which would you rather have: $700 per month or $5,500 per month? (I will give you a few moments to try to make the right choice.)

Let me summarize what we just discussed!

Save Now?		Save Later!
43	Current Age	43
$3,100	Monthly Income Provided by 401(k) and Social Security	$2,000
-0-	Income from Investments Age 53–Age 62 ($2,400/month for 9 years)	$3,500
$3,100	Total monthly income at retirement	$5,500
$2,400	Mortgage & Debt Payments	-0-
$ 700	Monthly income to live on	$5,500

NOTE: Once you are out of debt and you begin investing, you will now maximize your 401(k) or 403(b) contributions. To simplify my illustration, I did not reflect it that way.

Let me take a moment and address the question of taxes. Will you pay a little bit extra in income taxes along the way? Sure you would. But do you think that amount is significant in light of the outcome?

I want to ask you the question I asked earlier. Have I convinced you to stop putting money into your 401(k) or 403(b) plan?

If you are totally serious about accomplishing your debt freedom in as short a time as possible, you might even consider giving up that dollar-for-dollar (100%) match on the first 3%, and use those funds to accelerate the process even faster.

Remember what I said. I will give you options so that *you* can make the best decision for you. If you decide to save a little along the way, but still accelerate your debts, it does not mean that you will fail. It just means you won't be moving as fast as you otherwise would if you didn't. You will succeed *if* you have had that change in thinking; the one that says, "I will *never* use credit again." Okay! Stop your 401(k) contributions and start accelerating even faster. You will be in a much better position when the time comes for you to retire.

11

How to Succeed with Your Vehicles

Financial success can take on two forms. There are those who "are" financially successful, and there are those who "appear" successful. The one that is most prevalent in the United States is what most people believe "is" true success, and that is appearing successful. Having it all (or rather, having the appearance that you have it all) is what causes most people to be a financial bust. We as Americans can put on a pretty good face and appear that we are truly successful—that we have got it made. We wear the nice three-piece suit, sport that Rolex, hop into that Lexus or BMW, drive to that big home alongside the golf course, and then panic as we begin to open our mail with all the bills in it. We have fooled all our friends, tricking them into thinking that we "are" successful, but when we talk with the person in the mirror who knows the real story, we admit we are not. Throughout this chapter, I want to help you see what it takes to become successful "indeed" and not just appearing successful. You might be surprised how easy it is to become successful "indeed" if only you will handle your vehicles correctly.

When a young person gets his or her driver's license, the first thing that goes through their mind, in most cases, is, "How long will it be until I can get my own car?" They might drive their folks older car for a while, but all the time the thoughts are on "when" they can get their own. The indoctrination for the new car began years ago when that child was first starting to watch television. Every other commercial is for a new car that can go fast. After a decade of propaganda, that you "must" get a new car if you want to be cool, the child has been properly brainwashed by the car industry, and a good used car just simply won't do. As the child progresses toward adulthood, that "need" for a new car is stronger than ever. Finally, having a good steady job, the young adult takes the plunge, because "it's *only* $400 per month, and besides, I am not buying it, I am leasing it." The commercials continue, and he is bombarded with the message that he needs another car, because his car is four years old and has over 70,000 miles on it, and he can get another one for only $450 per month. So, he trades it in, not recognizing that he still has a big balance. Pretty soon, his other spending habits add to the monthly hole, and eventually, the payment cannot be made.

I cannot tell you the number of times I have seen a person (couple) with a huge car payment (or two), along with all the other stuff. That hole is so deep, it seems there is no way out. It is really sad, but it happens all the time. It doesn't have to, if the young person has been taught this one simple rule: never, *never,* never buy a brand new car. Just to make sure you understood that, let me put that into English. In English, that means never. This principle is not limited to young people. This goes for anyone reading this book. Never buy a brand new car. I hear all kinds of excuses. But I have to have a safe vehicle. Or, we need this new van so our whole family can fit. Or, I need this new car for my business so my clients will think I am successful. Here's one I hear all the time. "I can get the new car with *zero* percent interest." (I will discuss this a bit later in this chapter.) Perhaps I should say it one more time. Never buy a brand new car. Never!

Why would I say this? It's very simple. The average new car will lose about half its value in the first four years. So, here's what I recommend. Buy a four-year old car. It probably still has some warranties left on it, the bugs are worked out, and you pay half price for it. I always have someone tell me, Bob, if you are buying a used car, you are buying someone else's problem. Let me just say, "No, you are not." Someone else gave up a perfectly good used car, because they wanted another new car. You say that a car with over 70,000 miles is on its last leg and will require a ton of repairs. Not necessarily! If you take care of it properly, it could run for miles and miles and miles. Most cars, yes even American cars, are designed to run for over 200,000 miles. If you change your oil every three thousand miles, the car will literally run forever. (Some suggest that the oil be changed every five thousand miles, but for the minor cost of an oil change and the benefits new oil provides, I choose to do it every three thousand.) However, the dealers do not want you to know that, so they bring out a new model every year and try to suggest that you "need" a new car. The "need" is really for you to buy a new car because the car dealer and the manufacture "need" to continue taking all your money through the monthly payments. (Remember, it's only $400 a month.)

The question comes up, if I am making a ton of money, I deserve a new car. If you are reading this book, you are probably not making a ton of money. If you do, you are probably spending more than you are making (as the average American spends 110% of what they earn). Most of us are driving vehicles to reflect to our friends that we have it made; we are successful, and my new Lexus reflects my success. If our goal is to live like the millionaires, we probably had better check to see what they drive. In their book, *The Millionaire Next Door,* Stanley and Danko, who surveyed over 700 self-made millionaires, discovered an interesting characteristic about them. Seventy-six percent of those surveyed said they were currently driving a *used* car.[1] I would imagine that their response, when asked why they were not driving a new car when they obviously could afford one, would be something like, "How do you think I got to be a millionaire?" If you keep buying new cars, chances are great that you will never become a millionaire.

Let me tell you about a few friends of mine. John Cummuta used to drive a gold Corvette. Every time he would pull up in front of someone who hadn't seen the car, the response was, "Wow, John, nice car!" The next time they would see him, the response was, "Hey, John, how's it going?" John finally decided it was not worth $550 per month for that one big "Wow, John, nice car." So John decided to trade one Vet for another Vet. He got rid of the gold Corvette and bought himself a white Chevette. And by the way, he paid cash for that one.

Another friend, Mel Wild, is totally out of debt—mortgage included. A few years ago (after he became debt-free), Mel was driving a 1987 Corsica with over 200,000 miles on it. One day he was driving to work in his suit, and he was stopped at a stoplight. Up next to him roars a BMW. This man, in his suit, was also on his way to work. He looks over at Mel, then gets this look on his face, and shakes his head like, "Hey dummy, what are you doing driving that old car?" Mel (again, he was totally out of debt) just looks at the man and smiles, and thinks to himself, "You know, *you* are the dummy, because the money you are putting into your car payment, I am putting into my mutual fund.)

Who are you trying to impress? Are you impressing anyone by driving that BMW? What does it take to drive a BMW? Not really very much. Just sign here, sign here, and sign here, and you can drive one too. Do you really want to impress someone? Here is an idea. In five or six years, walk up to that person and tell him you are "totally" out of debt, house included. Now won't that impress people? Let me ask you, "Who should you be trying to impress?" Should we not be trying to impress the Lord with our proper stewardship? Our goal should not be to hear, "Hey, John, nice car," but rather, "Well done, good and faithful steward."

Have you seen those ads on television, which say, "Now you can drive a brand new BMW for only $399 per month."? (By the way, I have heard that BMW stands for "Both Must Work.") Your first thought is: "Wow, just $399 per month, I can afford that." But then the television flashes up six paragraphs of little print that you could not read even if you wanted to. Let me tell you what those six paragraphs say. First, you are entering a lease agreement. Second, you must pay $2,000 down. Third, you pay for the car for the next three or five or seven years. Fourth, you then have a residual payment of $15,000 or $20,000 in order to buy the car outright. Fifth, you have extra payments for excess mileage. Sixth, you have extra fix-up charges. However, if you do not want to make the residual payment or extra mileage and fix-up charges, they can be avoided by just getting another new car (with a new lease agreement and six more paragraphs).

I want to say something that might shock you. Never, *never, never* lease a car. What! My accountant says it's a good deal. Well, I say it is not. When you are leasing a car, you are renting a car. Do you want to rent a car? Go to Hertz or Avis, because you can get out of those anytime you want to. Dave Ramsey calls an automobile lease by a different name. He calls it a "fleece." I think that more accurately describes what really takes place when you sign those papers. I cannot tell you how many times I have heard people say they are paying $600 a month for a car that is parked in their garage because they have exceeded the mileage allowed. I have heard many times how people cannot afford the residual payment, so they are stuck with a new lease. I have heard other horror stories as well. I think these scenarios qualify this as a "fleece." They should be avoided at *all* costs. Never lease a car. Never!

I want to say something right here to encourage you. If you have made a mistake recently and bought a brand new car or just leased a car, do not beat yourself up. You didn't know. But now you know. So, when you get the car loan or lease paid off, never do it again. By the way, if you have just leased a car, I would recommend that you begin right now saving money to either make the residual payment at the end of the lease or to buy another car outright so you can turn the car back in. This will allow you to not get caught in the trap at the end of the lease.

Let's discuss my favorite. "But I can buy this new car for *zero* percent interest." Wow, that sounds pretty good, doesn't it? However, let me tell you what is really happening. You think the people at the dealership are good guys and they are looking out for your best interests. Wrong! They want to sucker you in to the showroom. By the time you get there, you have the new-car fever. You find just the right car and you are ready to sign the papers. But wait. Because of a few little blips on your credit report, you do not qualify for the zero percent interest. For you, it's only 9%. That's still a pretty good deal, right? So, not only are you into an overpriced new car, you are paying finance charges on top.

If you do qualify for the zero percent interest because of your great credit rating, you can rest assured you will not receive even one-nickel discount on that vehicle. The dealer has it priced to the max, and that's what you pay. Additionally, you pay a ton of phantom charges—things like freight from wherever, undercoating (whatever that is—I think it just means additional profit), and twenty-seven different warranties. But hey, it's zero percent interest.

Let me take you through a process, which is presented in the chart on the following page. I want to compare someone who buys a new car for $25,000 (after trade-in) and finances it at 0% interest with someone who buys a five-year old car for $12,500 and finances it at 10%. Both make payments of about $400 per month. After five years, both trade in for another newer car of similar cost and age. Here is what happens.

With the new car at zero percent interest, the payments will be $416 for five years (60 months). If you bought the used car for $12,500 at 10% interest, the payments would be $403 for three years (36 months). At the end of the three years, you could continue saving that $400 for the next two years, accumulating over $11,000 (at 10% interest *earned).*

At the end of the five years, you trade the car in and borrow another $25,000 at zero percent interest. Payments continue at $416 per month for the next five years. However, if you had saved $11,000, you could put that toward another used car ($12,500), leaving you a balance of $1,500 to finance at 10%. If you reached a little deeper into your pocket and made a payment of $507 (instead of $416) for three months, you would pay the car off in three months. You would then be able to save $416 for the next 57 months, accumulating over $30,000.

At the end of another five-year period, you repeat the process. That's right, another new car at zero percent interest with payments of $416. Or, you could pay cash $12,500 for another used car, leaving you an investment of over $17,000. Again, by saving the $416 each month for sixty months, you would accumulate over $61,000.

Let's do a quick summary. 1) Drive a new car (at zero percent interest) and get another new car every five years, or 2) Drive a used car for five years, and then trade it in for another used car every five years. At the end of the fifteen years, you would have: 1) Nothing, except a five-year old car, or 2) A ten-year old car, and $61,000 cash. Here are the two questions you need to ask yourself. First, which would your rather have? (Another tough question. I'll give you a few moments to answer it.) Second, how many people (including yourself) have you impressed over the years, and was it worth it?

Buy A Car At 0% Interest

New		**Used**
$25,000	Cost	$12,500
0.0%	Interest	10%
$416.67	Monthly Payment	$403.34
60 Months	Term	36 Months
$25,000	Total of Payments	$14,520
	Save	$416/mo. for 24 mo.
	Total Saved	$11,002

In Five Years, Buy Another Car

New		**Used**
$25,000	Cost	$12,500
-0-	Down Payment	$11,002
$25,000	Borrow	$1,498
0.0%	Interest	10%
$416.67	Monthly Payment	$507.68
60 Months	Term	3 Months
$25,000	Total of Payments	$1,523
	Save	$416/mo. for 57 mo.
	Total Saved	$30,194

In Ten Years, Buy Another Car

New		Used
$25,000	Cost	$12,500
-0-	Down Payment	$12,500
$25,000	Borrow	-0-
	Invest	$17,694
0.0%	Interest	
$416.67	Monthly Payment	
60 Months	Term	
$25,000	Total of Payments	
	Save	$416/mo. for 60 mo.
	Total Saved	$61,709

Let me give you another scenario. This one is actually *better,* because it involves *no debt* at all.

Step 1: Instead of buying that good used car in the previous illustration, put your vehicle wants on hold for a year. Start saving that $416 per month now, and at the end of one year, you will have $5,000.

Step 2: At the end of that first year, buy a good used vehicle for $5,000. You can find a pretty nice used car for $5,000, but you must look hard and not buy the first thing that pops up. Keep saving that $416 per month. At the end of the second year, you will have that used $5,000 car and another $5,000 in cash.

Step 3: You can now upgrade and buy a $10,000 used vehicle, paying cash and trading in your first vehicle (which will still be worth about $5,000). Continue saving $416 per month for another year.

Another twelve months later you will have that used $10,000 vehicle, plus another $5,000 in cash.

Step 4: You can upgrade further and now buy a $15,000 used vehicle, paying cash and trading in your second vehicle. Continue saving $416 per month for another year, and twelve more months you will have that $15,000 used vehicle, plus another $5,000 in cash.

Step 5: Continue upgrading until you have a vehicle that will meet your needs (or wants). Keep saving that $416 per month, because it has become a habit. You will now be able to pay cash for any vehicle you want. Now take that monthly savings and add it to your debt elimination plan (or to your wealth building plan if you have eliminated your debts totally).

In summary, let me say that buying your vehicles wisely *can* make you succeed financially, but buying them improperly *will* make you fail financially.

Never, *never, never* buy a brand new car, and never, *never, never* lease a car.

Again, the choice is yours.

[1] Thomas J. Stanley & William D. Danko, The Millionaire Next Door, Atlanta, GA, Longstreet Press, 1996, page 113.

12

Credit Cards & Consolidation Loans

I have mentioned before that we do not need any more credit cards, because we will *never use credit again.* Therefore, I recommend that you cut them up and get rid of them. All of them! Yes, even that one you got when you were back in college. This should be relatively simple to do. You just need to perform plastic surgery. Get out the shears, and one by one begin cutting them up. If you are struggling, thinking that you cannot possibly cut up that department store credit card, I have a suggestion. Think what life would be like with *no* payments—no mortgage payment, no car payment, no student loan payment, and yes, even no credit card payment. I have just described for you something that has been elusive so far, and that is *freedom.* Think about this freedom, and then cut those cards, even the one that you might be emotionally attached to. Remember, as I said earlier: No Payments = Freedom.

I can hear some of you saying, "But I have to have a credit card for emergencies." If that is you, let me put your mind at ease. Keep one just for an emergency, but cut up all the others. You do not need them. However, I do not want you to keep that one "emergency" credit card in your wallet or your purse. If you do, "emergencies" will happen and you will pull out the card; emergencies such as, "oh it's late and I don't want to cook and then do dishes. Let's eat out!" That is not an emergency! Emergencies like, "I have got to get that new golf club to improve my game." Again, that is not an emergency. Here's the deal. If you keep one credit card for emergencies, you must follow my advice. Cut up all your credit cards, except one. Take that one credit card and put it in an envelope. Then, go outside, open your garage door, open the trunk of your car, lift up the spare tire, and slide the envelope under the spare tire. Then, put down the spare tire, close the car trunk, close the garage door, and there you have it. You have that credit card for that unexpected emergency.

Ladies, I can assure you that if you are at the mall, and you see that new dress or those new shoes, you are not going to think to yourself—Emergency, Emergency. You will not run out to your car, open the trunk of the car, lift up the spare tire, pull out the envelope, and get your credit card and then run back in. What will happen as you are running out to the car is that common sense will have a chance to set in, and you will be reminded about your goal of getting out of debt. All of a sudden, you will be returned to what's really important. It's not the dress or the new shoes. It's about your goal of becoming debt-free in a short period of time. What you have just done is that—as a long-time friend, Carol Craigie, used to say—you have "tricked yourself" into being successful, and we must do that if we are to succeed.

I can hear you men as you read this saying, "Yeah, ladies. Don't do something foolish like buying dresses or shoes, because that will ruin our budget." But before you point the finger too much, I want to remind you guys that we are just as bad in this area, if not worse, because we are after that new golf club or the new power tool. Those "emergencies" are not really as important to us if we have to run through this process of hustling to the car to get that credit card. Again, common sense will have a chance to settle in.

You say you have to have one credit card that you use "as a convenience." You say you use it to make reservations on-line, or you use it to rent a car. You use it so you don't have to carry cash. You use it to avoid the lines at the movie theatre and you buy your ticket outside at the machine. You use it to get fast food. I have heard all the "excuses" for having to carry a credit card, and I don't buy any of them. You *do not* need a credit card, period. People all the time are telling me, "Bob, we live in a plastic world. We have to have a credit card." I say, "No!" Well, how then do you do all those things I mentioned above?

Let me tell you what I do. I have two Visa cards: one for my personal use and one for my business. But I need to tell you. These are *not* credit cards.

They are debit cards. With a debit card, I can do anything you can do with a credit card—I can make reservations, I can purchase items on-line, I can get into the movie theatre (I can even use it to buy popcorn inside), I can use it at the fast food restaurants. One thing I cannot do with the debit card that you do with a credit card is—pay interest. I cannot pay interest with my card, because every time I use it, I have to make an entry into my checkbook. It may also be called a Check Card. Using the debit card is just like writing a check. I am not getting credit; I am simply spending my money. The second thing I cannot do with the debit card that you can do with the credit card is to spend more money than I have. Again, if you do not have money in the bank, you cannot use the debit card, because it will be refused. Let me say this very clearly. *If you are committed to getting out of debt, you do not want to spend more than you have.* You do not need a credit card, period. Keep one for an emergency, if you really feel you need to, and then get rid of *all* of the others.

If your bank does not offer a debit card, let me be right up front here. Find a bank that does. It is that important to your success to have a debit card and never use a credit card. One thing to be "very careful" about when you get that debit card, *do not* get overdraft protection tied to it. That is simply credit, and it encourages free spending. Remember, we will *never use credit* again.

I have heard many, many people say, "Oh, I use a credit card as a convenience and pay it off at the end of the month." I have also heard many say, "But I can get a rebate of 5% for every dollar that I spend on my credit card." I might be tempted to say that's okay, but it is not okay, because various studies have shown that people who use credit cards spend at least 35% more than those who spend cash. So think about this: You spend an extra 35% and you get a 5% rebate. Any way you look at it, you are out of pocket at least 30%, if not more. If you think this is still a good idea, you had better pull out your calculator and check the numbers. It is *not* a good idea. I have heard many others say, "But Bob, I can earn airline miles with my purchases." I have two responses to that one. First, you still spend an extra 35% + to get those miles. You could simply pay cash for your purchases and use that 35% to buy airline tickets. In fact, you could probably travel around the world a few times with what that 35% would amount to over a few years. Second, you cannot travel anywhere, because you are broke and don't have any money. You are living paycheck to paycheck and even though it hasn't cost you much to fly, the only way you could get money to spend while you are away is to use the credit cards, and remember, we are not going to do that anymore. If you want to use your credit card and pay it off at the end of the month, and get that 5% rebate or those airline miles, do this: use your credit card to buy things in your "written" budget.

(You do have one, don't you.) That way, you will not spend 35% more. In fact, you won't spend 1% more.

The easiest way to succeed is to just admit this: Credit cards (or rather the abuse of the credit cards) have caused you to fail. It isn't working and something has got to change. *Stop* doing things your way, and try them my way for a change. You will be surprised when it works.

Let me share with you why you shouldn't use credit cards and let me challenge you to try something. Years ago, my son, Brandon, turned 16, and he did what every 16-year old young man did. Do you think he wanted to buy a car? Well, not my son. He was too smart for that. He wanted to drive my car. "Dad, let me borrow the car and run those errands for you." "Let me borrow the car so I can drive to school." "Let me borrow the car and drive to youth group." Okay, son, here are the keys. One day, our family was sitting in church, and the pastor was just getting ready to dismiss us. Brandon leaned over to me and whispered, "Dad, let me have the keys. When we are dismissed, I will go out and get the car and pull it up front. You and mom can visit with people like you always do, and then when you come out, I'll be right there and we can hurry home." You see, the Denver Broncos were playing an early football game, and he wanted to see how they were doing. I said, "okay."

After church, as we were visiting with a couple, I saw Brandon walking back into the church with his head hanging low. When I asked him what was wrong, he told me that he had hit a car. He had backed into another car in the parking lot, and we found out it would take $420 to fix it. He got this sheepish look on his face and said, "Dad, what are you going to do?" I looked at him and responded, "Brandon, I was not driving. What are *you* going to do? When he finally figured out I was not going to let him off the hook, he finally said, "Okay, Dad, take the money out of my account." I want you to know that Brandon had been working since about age 12, mowing lawns, shoveling snow, working odd jobs, and he had built up a pretty good savings account. I told him we (he and I) would take care of things together. We went to the bank on Monday, and the teller asked him if he wanted a cashier's check or cash. He said he wanted a check. I told her, "Give him cash." She asked if he wanted large bills, and he said, "yes." I told her, "Give him 20's." She gave him $420 in 20's and we drive over to the gentleman's house. Brandon says, "Mr. Rose, I am so sorry for hitting your car; here is the money." I asked Brandon to count it out. So, here was my 16-year old son counting out the money. Twenty ... Forty ... Sixty ... Do you think he knew the value of a twenty-dollar bill? He had worked nearly five hours to get *one* twenty-dollar bill. Now, he was giving away a whole stack of them.

I want to ask you a very sobering question. What about *you?* You have worked hard—you have given up part of your life—for that twenty-dollar bill. But how easy is it to pull out that credit card, slap it on the counter, and say, "Charge it." It's only ninety dollars. "Charge it." It's only two hundred dollars. "Charge it." It is so easy to use that card, isn't it? It is even easy to pull out a debit card and slap it down. It is even easy to write the check: two hundred dollars.

I want to challenge you "right now" to do something you have never done. Put away the credit cards (oh, wait, I forgot—you don't have them anymore, because you cut them up), put away the debit card, put away the checkbook, and for the next two weeks, carry cash. I can assure you when you have to pull out a twenty-dollar bill, you will stop to think about for a moment. If Andrew Jackson is staring at you, you don't want him to leave. It's even harder with Ulysses Grant ($50 bill) or with Ben Franklin ($100 bill). I will guarantee right now that you will think twice before you let them depart from your wallet or purse. You will begin to look at money from an entirely different perspective than you presently do. Try this for two weeks. If it has no impact in the way you handle money, then go back to your old way (which has not worked very good so far).

The first step in getting out of debt is simply: no new debt. This is not rocket science. As I stated before, no new debt means *no new debt.* For those of you who may not understand what I am saying right now, let me translate that into English. If you are in a hole and you want to get out—stop digging! I hope you got it that time.

I counsel couples from time to time. They come in with a list of all their debts and the first thing I tell them is to stop using their credit cards. Most of the time their response is, "We cannot do that." But they must, and *you* must also. If you really want to get out of the financial hole that you have dug for yourself—stop digging. Put away the financial shovel. Get rid of the credit cards. You can make it through life without them. Your grandparents did.

Let me interject something right here. Just when we thought credit cards have gotten as bad as they could, now they have gotten even worse, because now *they are going after our children.* If you were to go to any college or university, you would be able to find dozens of places where a new college student can get a credit card. "Sign up here and get a free T-shirt (or water bottle or Frisbee)." Our children go away to college and now they may be thinking about making decisions on their own. They are enamored by the free T-shirt and they think the card will give them some status. Some (who have not been taught by their parents) even think it's *free* money, at least until the bill comes. Now our children have the card, and they can get all the things *now* that their parents have (although it took the parents 20–30 years to get them).

I have even heard that many High Schools now offer credit cards. Rather than offering credit cards, I believe they should be offering classes on finances.

I want to ask you a series of three questions: 1) Are the schools teaching our children good money habits? For the most part, I can answer, "No," they are not. 2) Are the churches today teaching our children good money habits? Again for the most part, I believe the answer is No. 3) Are we, as parents, teaching our children good money habits? From my experience, I believe the answer again, for the most part, is No. Since our schools, our churches, and we as parents are not teaching our children good money habits, the question becomes, "Who is teaching our children?" The answer might surprise you. Madison Avenue says, "We will teach your children." And so they do. Our children again go into debt bigger, deeper, and faster than we ever thought possible, because they want all the stuff and they want it now.

Let me tell you, parents. We *must* teach our children about money. We must educate them on the trap that the credit industry has set for them. I have heard many parents say that they want to teach a child about a credit card, and they get them one while still in high school. I must say at this point, I believe that is like a father handing his child a metal fork and pointing him/her to an electrical outlet. It is dangerous. I believe we must teach them, but let them learn from our mistakes and see the danger without experiencing it themselves. When a credit card application comes for you in the mail, why not pull it out and sit with your son or daughter and go through the terms. Explain to them the interest that must be paid (even though it might only be 3%). Explain late charges, over-limit fees, transfer fees. Make it a good teaching time. We must teach our children about money. Larry Burkett once said, "We are not teaching children; we are teaching future adults.

Let me share two Scriptures with you. Proverbs 22:7 states, "The rich rules over the poor and the borrower becomes slave to the lender." We have already looked at this verse. The verse just prior, Proverbs 22:6, states, "Train up a child in the way he should go. Even when he is old he will not depart from it." I just wonder if God put those two verses side-by-side for a reason. Let me give you my translation of those two verses: "Train up a child not to be a slave." *We must* teach our children about money.

Consolidation Loans

We have talked about credit cards and how we must get rid of them. But, I often hear people say they can consolidate their payments, and that will help them out. A consolidation loan is where you borrow money from one place to pay off two or three or ten other debts that you have. In most cases, a company will not loan you money for a consolidation loan unless you have some collateral—something that you own that they can sell to repay your loan if you fail to make the payments. Collateral may consist of your paid-off car, your savings or investment account, or equity in your home. When you get a consolidation loan by using the equity in your home as collateral, this is typically called a 2nd mortgage or a HELOC (Home Equity Line Of Credit).

There are a few reasons being touted as the truth for getting a consolidation loan, but I want to warn you, *consolidation loans do not work.* The first reason you might be told to get a consolidation loan is to lower your monthly payments. Let's think about this. If your payment is lowered, but the balance remains the same, there is a good chance you will stay in debt longer. The second reason you are told is that the interest rate could be lower. I want to say something that I have said before. We do not have an interest rate problem, we have a cash flow problem. Getting a consolidation loan is probably not the best thing for you, if interest rate is your only concern. The truth is that many consolidation loans get you deeper in debt. There may be additional charges by the bank or mortgage lender added to your balance. Also, here is something I have seen often. As you are applying for that loan, the question comes up, "Do you need an extra $5,000 for that new deck on your house?", or "Do you need $3,000 for that much needed vacation?" Too many times people increase their debt simply because someone has put an idea in their head, and they think they deserve that vacation or that new thing.

I want to say very loud and clear that *consolidation loans do not work* because they do not address the real reason you got into debt. In my counseling sessions, I have couples in my office with a list of their debts. Many times I see a mortgage, a car loan (or two), a consolidation loan, and a long list of credit cards. I ask them what the consolidation loan was for, and their response is, "Oh, we used that to pay off our credit cards." When questioned about the long list of credit cards, they respond, "Oh, we charged them back up again." I am sure if this does not describe you, it describes many of the people you know.

Am I saying to never take out a consolidation loan? No, I am not. But let me ask you this question: If you got a consolidation loan three months ago and you saved three hundred dollars a month, where is that three hundred dollars now? Most people shrug their shoulders and say, "Gee, I don't know." Well, I do! It was used to buy something for $300 per month. But, what if you decided to get a consolidation loan next week and you could free up three hundred dollars a month. What will you do with that three hundred dollars? (I hope at this point you will say that you will add it to your accelerator to eliminate your debt even faster.)

Let me finish this section by saying something that you might want to highlight or underline or circle. The purpose of a consolidation loan (or a re-finance of your home for that matter) should *never* be to lower your monthly payment. Instead it should be to lower the amount of time you have left to pay.

Before you get a consolidation loan, re-read that last paragraph. *The purpose of a consolidation loan should never be to lower the amount of your monthly payment. Instead it should be to lower the amount of time you have left to pay.*

13

The Mortgage Trap

Many Americans have a mortgage, and many others do not yet have a mortgage, but wish they did. Home ownership used to be part of the American Dream. Couples would get married; the husband would get a job, with the hopes of working 40+ years for the same employer; they would begin a family, and over time (typically 30 years or less), they would pay the house off. Most homeowners would eventually own their own homes—free and clear—and have the security of knowing that whatever happened in the world—wars, economic collapses, job layoffs, etc.—they would have their own house to live in. My, how times have changed. There is no longer the trend where there is only one income. Jobs do not last 40 years, like before. And, most people do *not* own their own homes.

In a typical workshop on how to get out of debt, I ask the question, "How many of you own your own home?" Not surprisingly, about 75% of the hands go up. Then I ask the question, "How many of you own your own home—with the bank?" Again, not surprisingly, the same 75% of the hands go up. If we were to turn the clock back a few generations, we would see that most people owned their own homes independent of the banks.

Let me ask you this question. Do you know where the word "mortgage" comes from? It comes from two Latin words. The first word "mortuus" is the Latin word for "death." You know, mortuary, mortician, mortality. It literally means "death." Next is the Latin word "gage," which means "pledge" or "grip". The word "mort-gage" literally means "death grip."

I know you are chuckling out there, but let me explain further. In the Get Out of Debt workshop, I mention that 20% of our lifetime income will go toward mortgage interest—not mortgage payments, but mortgage interest. If we make one million dollars over our lifetime, 20% is $200,000. I know you are still chuckling, so let me put it into English. If you have a $100,000 mortgage (that's really low for the Denver area), and you pay the mortgage off over 30 years, at 9%, you will have paid nearly $190,000 in interest. That's nearly twice what you borrowed. Adding this to the $100,000 principal, you will have paid nearly $300,000 for that $100,000 home. When you buy a house you think, "It's going to cost me a ton of interest," but you don't stop to think about what a ton is. Nearly $190,000 interest, plus the $100,000 principal is what you will pay. That is nearly $300,000 of your hard earned wealth for that $100,000 home. That *is* a death grip.

At this stage, I get two responses. First I hear, "Yeah, Bob, but my house will appreciate." In Colorado, it probably will. But will it triple? The second thing I hear is, "But Bob, I get to write off the interest on my taxes." That's true, you do, but as I'll discuss in a later chapter, that's conventional wisdom and conventional wisdom does not work. That's the bad news. You pay three times what you borrow over that 30-year period.

But, it gets worse. Consider Uncle Sam! He gets one-third of everything you earn. You need to earn $450,000 to net $300,000 to pay for that $100,000 home. I'm telling you, it's a death grip.

But, it gets worse. You see, the average American moves every 7.1 years and refinances every five years. Let me ask you. Have you moved in the last 7 years? Have you refinanced in the last five years? When you move or refinance, what you are actually doing is starting over. Another 30 years is staring at you. Not only that, but you have added to your mortgage in origination fees and closing costs. Also, it is highly likely that if you refinanced, you took out funds for that new deck or that vacation, and your new mortgage is a lot higher than the old one. *Do you know that the average Americans who move or refinance every seven years will never own their own home?* Are you getting the picture? Unless you make a change *now,* you will not be able to escape the jaws of the Death Grip. Well, let me expound a little further.

You buy a home and your monthly principal and interest (P & I) payment is $1,000. You know—$950 for principal and $50 for interest, isn't that right? Yeah, I wish. You and I both know it is $950 for interest and $50 for the principal. Okay, you have been in your home for five years. You have made 60 monthly payments. You have now reduced that $100,000 mortgage all the way down to $94,000. Your $1,000 payment is now $100 principal and only $900 interest. You are finally starting to make some progress.... And then you move or refinance. If you move, it is usually to a larger house. If you refinance, it usually includes additional origination fees, closing costs, and cash out for that basement construction or vacation. And the worst move you can make is to take out another 30-year loan. Now your monthly principal and interest payment is $1,200, which is $1,150 for interest and $50 for the principal.

I hear people say all the time, "But, Bob, I got a good rate." I am only paying 4% interest." Hear me closely when I say this. It is not a 4% loan unless you pay it off in one year or over the full 30 years. How many people do that? Very, very few! If you move or refinance often, and take out a new 30-year loan, it's not a 4% loan. It is a 95% loan, because 95% of your money is gone to someone else *forever.*

So, what is the answer? I simply say that if you have been in your house for five years and you move or refinance your home, you should get a 25-year loan. Wow, I can hear the screams coming in already. But,

Bob, with a 25-year loan, I could not afford the payments on that new house. If you cannot afford the payments, I recommend that you strongly consider not moving. If you are refinancing, you can afford those payments, because if you refinance *only* what you currently owe, your principal and interest payment will pretty much be the same. If you have a $100,000 mortgage at 7%, your principal and interest over 30 years will be $665. After five years, your balance has dropped to $94,000. If you were to refinance that $94,000 at 7% over 25 years, your principal and interest payment would be $664. If the interest rate were lower, the payment would be lower still. You *can* afford it, but you have to fight the temptation to pull money out for stuff or to go with a slightly lower payment over 30 years. By doing this, you *will* pay your house off over 30 years and you will be in the 2% of people in the U.S. who actually own their own home. You can do it, but like I've said before, you have to want to do it.

However, I have a *better* idea for you. If you are buying for the first time, or moving, or refinancing again, I would recommend two things before you decide to sign the papers. First, I would suggest that you get no more than a 15-year mortgage. What! How can you say that, Bob? I could never afford that payment. Yes you can, and you should make sure you can do it, or else don't move or don't refinance or don't buy your first house. You can afford it, because if you want to turn a 30-year loan into a

15-year loan, you do not need to double the payment, as I have heard some suggest. You will need to add approximately 25% more of the principal and interest (P & I) payment. If your principal and interest were $1,000 for a 30-year loan, you would need to increase your payment about 25% (or $250) to $1,250 and now you have a 15-year loan. If things are so tight that you cannot even consider adding $250 to the 30-year loan payment, then you would be well-advised to not make the move. Stay where you are. Don't move to that larger house. Be content with your current house, or else look in a different neighborhood for that larger (and less expensive) house.

The second recommendation is to make sure that your monthly mortgage payment be less than 25% of your net income. Remember, net income is your take-home income. Anything more than 25% means that you are buying too much house for your income. Too many problems can arise when a person or couple buys a house right to the edge of their income. A few things happen and now they cannot afford the payments and they eventually lose the house. Make sure you buy the right amount of house in the first place, and you will not have to deal with the problem when the unexpected occurs. As the saying goes, when you are making purchases, especially large purchases like a house, make sure you "act your wage."

Let me tell you about a new gimmick. It is called an interest only loan, and it *is* a gimmick. What this means is that for a certain period of time, you will pay interest only on the loan. The balance of the loan stays the same, because there has been no principal payment. The benefit that is "sold" with the loan is that payments are lower and you can get "more" house. You move into the house with good intentions to pay some principal, but then each month there are "emergencies" that keep you from making those additional payments, or you just have to get that new thing. "But next month, I'll make payments. I promise." Next month comes and there is another excuse why you could not. Good intentions will not pay off a house. Only extra principal payments will.

Another danger is the Adjustable Rate Mortgage, or A.R.M. This means the rate of interest that you pay can vary every year, every quarter, or every month, depending upon the contract you signed, which means the amount of your payment can vary every year, every quarter, or every month. With rates currently near a 40-year low, it makes *no* sense to save 1/2% or even 1% with an A.R.M., because the rates can only go one way, and that's up. You may save now, but next year and the next year, you could be paying more than if you had locked in a fixed interest rate. Stay away from Interest Only Loans or Adjustable Rate Mortgages. If you currently have one, I would strongly suggest that you try to lock in a fixed rate before the rates go too high.

Only a very small percentage of people reach retirement with their homes paid off. Are you going to be one of them and have the security that whatever happens, you will own your home? The choice is yours. But you have to start today.

14

What About Emergencies?

One of the biggest mistakes I see as people try to eliminate their debts is their own thinking about emergencies. They get excited about getting out of debt, begin pursuing their plan ... and then an emergency happens. There are two things we need to know before we begin this plan. First, emergencies *will* occur. Life seems to be full of emergencies, doesn't it? Things seem to be running smoothly and then life happens—the kids get sick, the refrigerator breaks down, company comes into town with their large appetites—and it seems the best laid plans begin to fall apart. We need to plan for emergencies, because they *will* happen.

The second thing we need to know is that when emergencies happen, we must not let them detour our plan. Many people say they were cruising along on their debt elimination plan, an emergency happened, and, just like that, they detour. They throw in the towel. Many go back to using the plastic to address the detour. Stop! Wait! Don't do that. I want you to look at an emergency not as a detour, but as a speed bump. A detour means you leave the desired path. A speed bump, on the other hand, simply causes you to slow down, go over the bumps of the emergency, and then continue on, resuming full speed ahead. If you know that emergencies are going to occur before you start, and you have a game plan for how to address them before they happen, then you can handle the speed bump, rather than deviate from your desired course.

It's important that you determine ahead of time what an emergency actually is. Going out to dinner after working a long day is not an emergency. A skiing trip with your friends is not an emergency. A new computer, simply because you want the latest features is not an emergency. (If your computer fails and you need one for your work, then it might be considered an emergency, but if it is just so you can "surf the net," then it probably is not.) These items—going out to dinner, a skiing trip, upgrading your computer—are things that, if you want them, you should build them into your monthly budget.

So, how then do we handle emergencies? It's really pretty easy. Just follow these simple steps. First, remember from Chapter Nine, we have developed up-front an emergency fund of $1,000. This one thousand dollars should handle most minor emergencies that come up. If your hot water heater goes on the blink, simply pull the funds from your bank or money market account, pay for a new hot water heater with cash, and now, it's no longer an emergency, but rather a little inconvenience. *Be sure* when this happens to take all accelerator funds next month to build that fund back up to $1,000, because there *will* be another emergency in the future and you don't want to get caught without an emergency fund in place.

Second, if the emergency is larger than $1,000, you simply go back to making minimum payments on all your debts, rather than accelerating one of them. This amount that you were using to accelerate your debts will range anywhere from $300 to $2,000, based upon where you are in the debt elimination process. If you have just begun the program and you have not yet paid off any debts, then the total *accelerator* is just the 10% of monthly gross income that we found in Chapter Nine. However, if you are a couple years in, and several debts have been paid off, then your *accelerator* could be $500, $1,000, or maybe $2,000. If you are nearing the end, this amount could be much higher still. These numbers are based upon the amount of debts you started with and the amount of monthly payments that you have freed up so far along the way.

Over the years, I have met people who have over $30,000 in credit debt. Others have over $60,000 in credit debt. I have met several with credit card debt over $120,000! When I ask them how all this happened, the usual response is: "Oh, I lost my job and my spouse got cut back to half-time, and we had to live on our credit cards. A year later and I still am not employed with the same income as then." I want to say one thing *loud and clear.* Please do not miss this. When an emergency occurs, it all comes down to two words: Master Card! Yes I said two words. Not MasterCard, but Master Card! When you have that emergency, you can depend upon the Master, or you can depend upon the Card. All too often, an emergency strikes and the first thing we do is to reach for our plastic. I have to take care of that emergency. At this point, I want to say: *"Wait! Don't do that!"*

God promises to meet our need and when an emergency happens and we reach for the credit card, He allows us to handle things ourselves. God is seeing our emergency and waiting to see how we will respond. When we pull out the card, God is saying, "I wanted to meet that need for them, but their trust is in the Card, so they don't need Me." We must turn to the Lord in the event of an emergency. Trust in the Master and not in the Card. He *will* meet our needs, just as He has promised.

What if your emergency is a medical emergency? If you suffer a major medical crisis, after the dust has settled and the insurance company has paid their portion, then there is your deductible portion remaining. Maybe it is $500; maybe it is $5,000, or maybe your portion is $50,000. What normally happens is that doctors, hospitals, anesthesiologists, etc., will contact you and ask you to pay. Your response is that you don't have the funds. Their next response is likely to be, "We can take your credit card." At this point, your response should be, "I don't have any credit cards, because Bob told me to cut them up and I did." When this happens, you can ask them this one simple question. Since I cannot pay cash for this, and it is highly unlikely I will be able to accumulate this much cash in the next several months (or years) to pay you, would you consider accepting a smaller amount, if I could scrape the funds together? Most doctors, hospitals, anesthesiologists, etc., will negotiate a payoff if you are unable to make the full payment. Also, most of these medical people will not charge interest on the outstanding balances.

Let me share a true story. I was working with a couple in the Denver area who owed one of the hospitals over $42,000. This was their balance after insurance had paid its portion. This couple both had limited income. They got their budget and paycheck stubs together and brought them to the hospital administrator. After reviewing their situation, the administrator said, "If you will pay $240, the hospital will forgive the balance of the $42,000. True story.

However, knowing how people behave (or fail to behave), I know that not everyone who reads this book will do as I say and cut up their cards. At that point, when asked to pay their portion with their credit cards, they will look to find one card that has enough room under the maximum available balance to make this charge. What these people are saying is, "I want to pay the *entire* balance and I want the interest clock to begin ticking right now." Please, don't do that.

Make the changes. You can live without your credit cards.

Let's discuss what happens when your car breaks down or become unsafe. This is an emergency. (You should realize, however, that the car you are presently driving will need some repairs along the way and a monthly budget category should include auto repair.) When your car dies on the side of the road, I must admit you need a new car. What I mean by that, though, is not a "new" car, but a "new-to-you" car. At this point, you need to find a good used car that will get you and your family from here to there safely. You do not need a $15,000 used minivan or a $20,000 used SUV. What you need is reliable transportation. You can find a great used car for $3,000–4,000 or a great used minivan or SUV for $6,000– 7,000. Let me say this right now. You will have to *look hard* to find these vehicles, but they are out there. Ask around at work or at church or in your neighborhood if anyone is looking to sell their used vehicle. Check the internet and newspapers. You do not need all the fancy trim and DVD players and leather seats. These all cost money. What you do need, let me say this again, is a good used car that will get you and your family from here to there safely.

You might be saying that is good, but I do not have that amount of money laying around. What I would recommend you do first is to pray (and pray diligently and pray often) that God would provide you a vehicle, and then wait as long as you can. If you have two cars in your family and one of them bites the dust, it might be that you ride the bus for a while, or have your spouse drive you to work. I know it might not be convenient, but the Lord might be asking how serious you are about getting out of debt. It would be very easy to run out and get something, but I would recommend that you take your time. If a vehicle has not arrived and you absolutely *need* that vehicle to get to work, you might get a small loan with the idea that you are going to pay it off within one year (even if it means a short-term, part-time job to help get those extra funds). This is the *only* time, and only as a last resort, that I recommend that you borrow money for anything other than a house. Let me just state it one more time to make sure you understand what I am saying. If you have exhausted all other options and must have a new-to-you car, you might borrow that $3,000–4,000, with a game plan to pay that entire amount back within twelve months. That really should not be a big deal, because that's only $250–330 per month for that payment. If you need that extra job, remember, you can deliver pizzas or throw newspapers with that good used car that you had to have. Meanwhile, you are continuing to rapidly accelerate the rest of your debt elimination as we discussed in an earlier chapter.

I have discussed how to handle those emergencies as they arise. We have talked about those emergencies and how to accumulate a fund to handle them. Please notice, we are not talking about establishing a six-month cash reserve. If we were to concentrate on building that six-month reserve, it could take three to four years to accumulate this reserve. Meanwhile, while paying debts first and having only an emergency fund of $1,000, after that 3–4 year period of time, you have paid off all debts except the house, and you are now half way through totally paying it off.

Once your house is paid off, you can now save all the funds that were going to debts (probably $2,000–$3,000 per month or more) and you can now fund that six-month cash reserve in about 2–3 months. You will not need the full six-month reserve as before, but you will only need about 30% of that, because—listen to me—over the last 5–7 years you have learned to live on 30% of your income. That 70% (or whatever the figure might be for you) has been coming in each month and going out to pay off debts. Once the debts are totally paid off, you do not need those funds, because you have learned to live without them. (See Chapter Ten for this discussion.) By the way, your $1,000 emergency fund as well as your six-month cash reserve should be kept in a bank savings account or a money market fund. Don't worry that you are not earning a lot of interest. The purpose of these funds is not to grow, but to provide for unexpected happenings. You want these funds to be easily available when you need them.

Now that we have discussed how to handle emergencies, let me ask you a question. How would you like to *avoid* emergencies? I already know the answer to that one. You would like to just like I would. Well, I have a way to help you avoid a lot of emergencies. Do you remember in Chapter Three when we discussed giving? I quoted from Malachi 3:10, which states, "Bring the whole tithe into the storehouse, so that there may be food in My house, and test Me now in this," says the LORD of hosts, "if I will not open for you the windows of heaven and pour out for you a blessing until it overflows." God says in verse 10 to bring the tithe. Then in verse 11, He states, "Then (after you have brought the tithe), I (God) will rebuke the devourer for you so that it may not destroy the fruits of the ground...."

In my early years of marriage, I remember vividly what my father-in-law told me. He said, "Bob, you can choose to give to the Lord or not give to the Lord. However, if you choose not to give, I believe God will allow Satan to come in and steal that money, with the kids getting sick or the car breaking down." As I have been teaching over the last fifteen years, I now recognize that this verse says exactly that. The best way for us to avoid emergencies is to be faithful in our giving.

Does that mean we will never experience an emergency? No, of course not! God uses emergencies in our lives to build our character. He uses emergencies to teach us perseverance. But, I believe the main reason God uses emergencies is to develop our trust in Him. We will still have emergencies in our lives, but they will be emergencies to develop us according to God's purpose; not those brought about by our own disobedience.

15

From a Consumer to a Steward

This chapter will give you some of the steps you need to take to bring this entire process to completion. I will address many behavioral issues, and again, I will make the recommendations, but you can make the decisions to either do them or not do them.

I want to discuss how to move from the consumer that Madison Avenue has made you to being the steward that God intended you to be. To begin, we need to define both a consumer and a steward.

A consumer, as you would imagine, is one who consumes. So then, let's define "consume." Webster gives the following definition, and as I am stating this, you must ask yourself if this describes you. To consume is "to take", "to do away with completely", "to spend wastefully", and "to squander." Let me ask you this: Do you like being called a consumer? Wow, I sure don't.

A steward on the other hand, according to Webster, is "one employed to ... keep accounts", "a finance officer", "a manager". Nowhere in this definition do we get the idea that a steward is an owner, simply a manager. When I think of a steward, I think of a corporate treasurer who has millions of dollars under his care, yet he owns "none" of them. He simply is a manager. That is one very important aspect of moving from a consumer to a steward. The consumer "thinks" that he owns it all and can use it however he wants. The steward "knows" he owns nothing, and he knows he has a responsibility for properly handling the resources.

I want to compare the consumer and the steward when it comes to handling money.[1] Look at the five items in the chart below and try to determine 1) where you are now, and 2) where you would like to be.

Let's look at each of these for a moment.

1) If the funds are not there, the steward either does without the item or waits until they have the money. What a concept! My parents used to call that "lay-away." They would save up until they had the cash, and *then* they would purchase the item. In today's language, it's called "Delayed Gratification." Wow, talk about a foreign idea. Everything is "Instant Gratification." I have to have it and I have to have it now. If you are a consumer, that is your mentality, but a steward will wait.

2) A consumer buys on impulse. Larry Burkett used to say that if you are considering a large item, there are three things you should do. First, compare prices, because prices vary tremendously from place to place.

Second, wait 24 hours. Walk away from the item and the urge will probably leave as well. Third, and guys, this is tough for us, are you in agreement with your spouse regarding this purchase? If not, do *not* buy it; it will only cause you trouble. I have added a fourth requirement before you make that large purchase. Can you afford to pay cash for the item? (I did not say, can you afford the monthly payment.) If you cannot afford to pay cash, then you need to utter the four toughest words in the English language: I cannot afford it!

Consumer		Steward
Buys items on credit. Not only pays exorbitant interest charges, but spends twice as much (112%) as someone who pays cash for purchases.	1	Buys everything with cash. Often receives a significant discount for using cash. If the funds aren't there, either does without the item or waits until they have the money.
Buys on impulse. In fact, their attic is full of last year's impulse purchases. These items either end up getting thrown away or sold at a garage sale for pennies on the dollar.	2	Plans purchase and considers impact on wealth-building goals. Buys items that "consumers" sell at garage sales for pennies on the dollar.
Spends every penny earned each month. Laments over the fact they aren't making enough money.	3	Lives on significantly less than they make. Saves a large portion of their income every month.
Influenced by adult peer-pressure (keeping up with the "Joneses.") Believes displaying social status is important to financial independence. Buys bigger home, new cars, expensive clothing—all to appear affluent and successful.	4	Believes true net-worth is more important than social status. Pays no attention to the "Joneses." All purchases are based on value rather than appearance. Also believes living a fulfilling, stress-free life is more important than Madison Avenue's version of success.
Spends little or no time on establishing a wealth-building/retirement plan. Plays the lottery in the desperate hope of striking it rich someday.	5	Spends significant amount of time planning financial future. Has specific wealth-building goals and sound investment plan to reach those goals.

Your neighbor might come knocking on your door and say, "Let's go skiing this weekend." You say to yourself, "I cannot afford it, but I do not want him to know that." So you pull out the credit card and say, "Okay!" *No,* don't do that. Tell your neighbor, "I cannot afford it." He will probably say, "You are right, I really cannot afford it either." You have just done him a huge favor. Get together for the weekend and spend time doing things that don't cost money.

3) The consumer spends everything he gets. The Bible calls that person a "fool." Proverbs 20:21 states, "The wise man saves for the future, but the foolish mans spends whatever he gets." The steward on the other hand has lived by the principle of spending less than he makes for a long period of time. This, according to Ron Blue, is the way to financial independence. Once the steward is out of debt, he/she can now save 30–40% of income, whereas the consumer cannot save even 2%.

4) The consumer is intent on keeping up with the Jones. He lives a life trying to impress and live the life-style of those around him. What he does not recognize is that the Joneses are going bankrupt faster that he is, because they are trying to keep up with the Smiths on the other side of them. The steward is not trying to impress anyone except the Lord with good stewardship of His resources.

5) The consumer is trying to get rich quick without work, while the steward is trying to get rich slowly with hard work and with a plan. The consumer is failing to plan; therefore he is planning to fail.

I am frustrated by the lure that Madison Avenue has set for us. We are continually bombarded by the ads on radio, TV, newspaper, and billboards (and now even movie theaters before the show).

Let me take a moment and tell you that the purpose of Madison Avenue advertising is to build discontent into our lives. These ads promise us that their product will give us the joy and the peace that our lives are lacking. *Let me be perfectly clear.* There is only one Source of joy and peace, and that is the Lord Jesus Christ, and please, do not let Madison Avenue tell you any differently.

I want to share a few more pitfalls that are waiting for those who are unaware. The Monthly Payment Trap is just that—a trap. Over the years we have been programmed to live monthly, to earn monthly, to spend monthly. The trap is simply to make "consumers" feel like they can afford this purchase. I cannot tell you the number of times I have counseled a couple buried by their finances. When they ask me how that happened, I simply look at a list of their debts and tell them, "Well, it was $20 per month for the palm pilot, and 'only' $39 per month for the cell phone and 'only' $50 per month for the gym membership and 'only' $95 per month for the new computer and 'only' $300 per month for her new car and 'only' $450 per month for his new truck. We fall into the Monthly Payment Trap without considering the total cost of the item. From this point forward, if you want to be a steward, you will not fall into that trap anymore.

Another large pitfall is that for only $1, you can have a chance to win several million dollars. That is called a "get-rich quick scheme," and should also be avoided. Let me just mention that there is a better chance that you will be struck by lightning than there is of winning the lottery. Proverbs 28:20 warns, "A faithful man will abound with blessings, but he who makes haste to be rich will not go unpunished." When I talk about accumulating $1.8 million after you have eliminated your debt, I am not talking about getting rich quickly. I am talking about getting rich slowly, but here's the key. I am talking about getting rich "open-handed." You see, the steward knows it is not his money, because everything belongs to the Lord. If the Lord knocks on the door of your heart and says to take $10,000 out of your 401(k), pay the tax and penalty and give the rest to your church building program, you had better do it—it's not your money.

Conventional wisdom tells us to do things, just because that is the way they have been done for a long time. Let me share the foolishness of some of these.

All the financial experts say we should pay ourselves first. I say we should eliminate debt first.

Financial experts say we should get cash-value insurance, because we are "renting" term insurance. I say we should rent our insurance for the short term that we will need it.

Your CPA may have told you, "Do not pay off your house, because you need the tax write-off." I want to put this one into English, just so you will see the foolishness. Do not pay off your house. Instead, give a dollar to the mortgage company so that Uncle Sam can give you a quarter. You see, the more you give a dollar, the more you get a quarter. The more you give a dollar, the more you get a quarter. The more you give a dollar, the more you get a quarter. There is only one word that I can think of for that...*stupid.* Do you want that tax write-off? Here is what you do. Pay off your house. Then give a dollar to your church. Uncle Sam will give you a quarter. But, if you do not want the tax write-off, here's a thought. Take that dollar, give Uncle Sam a quarter, and put seventy-five cents in your pocket. What a concept!

If we want to succeed financially, we must learn to live as stewards, not as consumers. It may take some time to learn these principles, but keep after them. Living as a steward is the only way to move from the *millstone* of debt to the *milestone* of debt-freedom. Now that you are debt-free, you can serve the Lord when, where, and how He wants. When the Lord calls you, your response will be, "Here am I, Lord; send me." *That is the real milestone.*

[1] Debt-Free & Prosperous Living seminar workbook, Page 5, used with permission. Debt-Free & Prosperous Living, Inc., Boscobel, WI

16

All Debts Paid-in-Full (Except One)

Well, there you have it. This is the process to get rid of *all* of your debts, *including your mortgage,* in about 5–7 Years. Okay, maybe in your case it's 10 or 11 (or maybe it's 2 or 3). In any case, this plan gets you out of debt faster than the one you had before you began this book. (You did have a plan, didn't you?)

I have shown you how to go through the Three Simple Steps to get out of debt. You recall what they were, don't you? Step number One—No New Debt. Remember, No New Debt in English simply means "No New Debt." Step Two, we use the Piggyback Principle. Once debt #1 gets paid off, we simply add those funds next month to debt #2, which means more money is going to debt #2, which means debt #2 will be paid off much sooner. Then we take the funds that were going to #1 and #2, and we add those to #3. That gets the typical American out of debt in 9–11 years. Step Three, we Accelerate. We find 10% of our monthly gross income to add to the debt elimination process. More money monthly means we get out of debt faster. Typically this will reduce the time frame from 9–11 years down to about 5–7 years. Great! Now you have done it and you are totally out of debt, including your mortgage.

Now you can begin saving as we discussed earlier, maximizing your 401(k) or your 403(b) plan. You can save in Roth IRAs. You should be able to save 30–40% of your income, whereas at the beginning you were not able to save even 3–4%. Saving at this rate will enable you, as Dave Ramsey says, to live like no one else.[1] You will be able to give like you have never dreamed of giving before. There will be *no* financial stress because you have no monthly payments, except the food and gas and basic living expenses. You might choose to have the spouse quit work. Remember what I said earlier: "No Payments = Freedom." Freedom to serve and give like you have always wanted to! You have finally reached the point we have been aiming for since you began. You have gotten rid of that *millstone* called debt and you have reached the *milestone* of debt freedom.

However, I would be remiss if I didn't tell you about another debt that you have. Maybe you didn't realize it, but there is more to debt elimination than we have discussed. Let me ask you what I consider to be *The Real Question.*

This question is what I consider to be the most important question you will ever ask yourself.

What does it matter if you get totally out of debt, then start accumulating wealth ... and then you lose your soul?

Let me share what I believe, and then, like I have said all along, you can decide what is best for you.

The Bible states that *all* of us have sinned. (Romans 3:23) We have all fallen short of perfection. Have you ever told a lie (even a little one)? That is a sin. Have you ever taken some paper clips or tablets from your employer for your personal use? That is a sin. Have you ever gossiped about a friend or family member? That is a sin.

We *all* have sinned.

The Bible goes on to say that the wages (or payment) for *a* sin (even one little sin) is death. (Romans 6:23)

We have all sinned and the penalty (the required punishment for that sin) is death. Wow! That is *bad* news.

However, the Good News is that Jesus came to earth, lived a perfect life without sin, and *He* paid our sin debt. He died in our place. He has given us a *free gift.*

Someone once said, "I owed a debt I could not pay. Jesus paid a debt He did not owe." That truly is Good News.

Do you know what a gift is? It is something that has been given to us for our benefit. However, the gift that Jesus gave is totally worthless to us ... unless we accept the gift. We must accept the fact that Christ paid our debt. We must trust that His payment (death) satisfied the debt and now the bill is "paid in full." We must accept Christ as our Savior (and Lord), and we must begin to live for Him.

You may not know exactly what that means, but if you have not accepted Christ as your Savior, and you want to talk about what you must do, I would recommend that you find a close friend who is a Christian. Have him/her explain what you must do to be saved. (The Bible, as usual, makes it very clear in this regard. Romans 10:9 states, "if you confess with your mouth Jesus as Lord, and believe in your heart that God raised Him from the dead, you will be saved.") Or, you could find a pastor of a Bible-believing church and have him explain it to you. Or, please feel free to contact me.

I would love to have the opportunity to share with you. (You can contact me through our website: www .bobmarette.com)

I want to leave you with four statements. If you are *not* a Christian—and you know if that's you—I want you to deeply ponder these four statements.

However, if you *are* a Christian, I want you to share these four statements with everyone you know who is *not.*

1) ***Heaven is a real place.***

The Bible talks a great deal about heaven.

Streets of gold (Rev. 21:21) And the twelve gates were twelve pearls; each one of the gates was a single pearl. And the street of the city was pure gold, like transparent glass.

No more tears (Rev. 21:4) And He will wipe away every tear from their eyes; and there will no longer be *any* death; there will no longer be *any* mourning, or crying, or pain; the first things have passed away.

Fellowship with God (II Corinthians 5:8) ... prefer rather to be absent from the body and to be at home with the Lord.

Heaven *is* a real place.

2) ***Hell is a real place.***

The Bible also talks a lot about hell.

Separation from God (I Corinthians 16:22) If anyone does not love the Lord, let him be separated from God—lost forever!

Weeping and gnashing of teeth. (Matthew 22:13) Then the king said to the servants, 'Bind him hand and foot, and throw him into the outer darkness; in that place, there will be weeping and gnashing of teeth.'

Eternal lake of fire. (Rev. 20:14,15) Then death and Hades were thrown into the lake of fire. This is the second death, the lake of fire. And if anyone's name was not found written in the book of life, he was thrown into the lake of fire.

Hell *is* a real place.

3) ***Eternity is a long time.***

In his great book on the joy of giving, Randy Alcorn talks about "the dot" and "the line."[1] Imagine a dot on the corner of this page. Then imagine a line extending out from that dot across the page, then continuing across the room, then continuing to the next room, then across the street, then across the city, then across the state, then continuing forever. Simply put, the "dot" represents our time here on earth. It has a beginning and it has an ending. The "line" represents eternity. The Bible makes it clear that Christians will spend eternity fellowshipping with God, with no more tears, and on streets of gold; and those who die without having received the gift which Christ has given will spend eternity in a lake of fire, separated from God forever, where there will be weeping and gnashing of teeth.

Eternity *is* a long time.

4) ***Jesus is the "only" answer***

I met a young man at Promise Keepers a few years back and he had a great T-shirt. In large letters it proclaimed, "JESUS IS THE ANSWER." Then, in much smaller letters underneath, it asked, "Now, what's the question?" Whatever questions or problems you might have, I want to say one thing: Jesus is the answer.

He is the answer to all of life. There are many, many books that will address this further. The Bible, from Genesis to Revelation, talks about Jesus and what He has done and what He is doing for you. I really appreciate the bumper sticker, which states:

> No Jesus, No Peace
> Know Jesus, Know Peace

Do you have peace in your life? If not, accept the *free gift* from Jesus and then develop a close relationship with Him daily. Remember the guarantee of success from page 19. No matter what happens in this world, you will experience a very real and lasting peace.

Again, let me encourage you. If you already know Christ, share these four statements with everyone you are acquainted with who does not. The Bible is the greatest *debt elimination* book ever written, because it addresses the Real Debt: the debt *you cannot* repay.

[1] Dave Ramsey, The Total Money Makeover, page footer

[2] Randy Alcorn, The Treasure Principle, Sisters, OR, Multnomah Publishers, 2001, page 48

Summary (Now What?)

Okay, now that I have given you the entire process and you know how to get out of debt, you might be asking, "Now what?"

I would recommend that you ponder Proverbs 16:3, which states, "Commit your works to the LORD, and your plans will be established." It does not say, your plans "might" be established. It does say "will" be established. The first step is to get with your spouse if you are married, or find a close friend if you are not. Bring this plan before the Lord. You might say something like this: "God, I am serious about getting out of debt. I am committing this debt-elimination plan to You. I need Your help. Forgive me for the way that I have used your money in the past. I want to become a steward of your resources, using wisely what You have given me. Please help me as I begin tithing and making the other choices that I must. Help me to be diligent. I am trusting You, Lord."

Then, begin the process.

1) No New Debt.
2) Piggyback
3) Accelerate

Then, be careful to listen to the Lord as He directs you.

Have you ever heard those motivational speakers who proclaim, "Knowledge is power. Knowledge is power." Over and over again they say it: "Knowledge is power." Well, I have a one-word answer for that: "Baloney." I say that because "K – A = 0 (zero)". You heard me, "K – A = 0." Think about that: "K – A = 0."

Knowledge Without Application Is Worthless.

Knowledge *is* Power, *only* when you apply what you have learned.

Do you know the difference between "ignorance" and "stupidity"?

Ignorance is "not knowing." There are many things that I am totally ignorant about: Chemistry, Computer Technology (ask my kiddos about this), Medicine, Auto Mechanics (my wife will agree here). I just do not know; therefore, I am ignorant. That's not a bad thing; it is just a fact.

Stupidity on the other hand is "knowing and not doing."

Before you began reading this book, you may have been ignorant. You may not have known. That was not a bad thing. It was just a fact.

But, now you know. (Now you do *not* have any excuses.)

What you have just done as you have read this book can be compared to a football game. You are the quarterback. You have just spent many hours, perhaps many days or weeks—in a huddle. That is the easy part. Now, it is time to break the huddle and run the play. That is the harder part—the execution of the play. But you *can* do it, if you follow the steps that were outlined in the huddle.

It is my prayer that you *will* apply the principles you have learned in this book. I pray that you begin the process of getting totally out of debt in a short period of time. I pray that you will be diligent in looking for that accelerator. I pray that you will succeed. Let me ask if you would please do me a favor? After you have gotten totally out of debt except the mortgage, and then again after you have totally paid off your mortgage, would you please contact me? Tell me *how* you did it. Tell me *how long* it took. Tell me the changes you made. Tell me the challenges you faced. I really want to know.

I would love to hear your story. Send me a letter or an e-mail.

Bob Marette
Financial Health Fair
P.O. Box 1081
Eastlake, CO 80614
bobmarette@hotmail.com
(Subject: TESTIMONY)
www.bobmarette.com

Appendix A

Net Worth Statement

	Value *(What does God own?)*	**Loans** *(What do I owe?)*	**Equity** *(Value minus loans)*
Cash on hand			
Checking Account			
Savings Accounts			
Mutual Funds			
Life Ins.Cash Value			
Home			
Other Real Estate			
Automobiles			
Furniture			

Jewelry	________	________	________
Business Valuation	________	________	________
Pensions	________	________	________
Retirement Plans	________	________	________
Credit Cards	________	________	________
Personal Loans	________	________	________
Student Loans	________	________	________
TOTAL*	________	________	________

* This represents your total Net Worth (Where are you currently?) This number will increase in one of two ways: 1) as you acquire more assets, and 2) as you pay off more debt. Your focus in the first several years should be increasing your net worth by eliminating all of your debt (mortgage included).

Testimonials

Bob Marette has taught this life-changing workshop—*How to Get Out of Debt in 5–7 Years, Including Mortgage, According to God's Principles*—at hundreds of churches around the United States. He has encouraged tens of thousands of God's people toward total debt elimination.

Here's what others say about Bob's teaching:

As a result of your teaching, my wife and I have seen blessing after blessing fall upon us and not only financially. The unity we enjoy over this issue is a blessing to our marriage.

> **Brian Thompson**
> Pastor of Congregational Life, Crossroads Church, Northglenn, CO

Bob does a wonderful job in communicating financial principles that can radically alter a couple's financial health.

> **John Stocker**
> Senior Pastor, Resurrection Fellowship, Loveland, CO

One gentleman remarked to me after the seminar he believed God was leading him and his wife to go up to 25% in total giving.

Jay Lindstrom
Associate Pastor, Sidney Evangelical Free Church, Sidney, NE

The seminar had all the components necessary to leave a lasting impact in the lives of the attendees.

Dave Reiter
Assoc. Pastor of Small Groups and Education, Orchard Road Christian Center, Greenwood Village, CO

You really helped me and my wife with some guiding principles for our finances. Thank you, Brother.

Donnie Dee
Southern California State Director,
Fellowship of Christian Athletes, Vista, CA

Bob brought us the good news of debt-free living. It is Biblically based, gives people hope, and was like a breath of fresh air.

Whaid Rose
Senior Pastor, Church of God (Seventh Day), Denver, CO

The seminar gave hope to many in our congregation who were deep in debt and discouraged. It gave them a plan to eliminate debt and a real hope to achieve debt-free living. The seminar was capped off with "the REAL question" regarding eternal matters.

Doug Klein
Senior Pastor, Faith Presbyterian Church, Aurora, CO

Here in Alaska practicality and reality-based teaching are very important! Bob shares both those values from a Biblical perspective! God speaks with authority and clarity through Bob and his gentle spirit of encouragement with grace and truth!

Chris Ball
Senior Pastor, Dimond Grace Church, Anchorage, AK

Getting the complete, step-by-step, month-by-month plan to get out of debt in 5–7 years was extremely uplifting and a positive beginning for many in our church.

Tim Hazelet
Chairman of the Deacons, First Southern Baptist Church,
Garden City, KS

Your genuine interest in helping people came across loud and clear. I believe every Christian should participate in this workshop.

Phil Largent

President, IMD International, Westminster, CO

I believe that your seminars are a necessity to bring about healthier finances for Christians in our country.

Jim Hamilton
Wyoming State Director, Fellowship of Christian Athletes,
Lander, WY

The week after you were here, the offering at New Hope was the single largest ever.

Paul Currier
Elder, New Hope Church, New Castle, CO

The emphasis was not only on how to become debt free, but also Biblical teaching on why it's so important to be debt free.

Steve Abbott
Senior Pastor, First Southern Baptist Church, Siloam
Springs, AR

Your seminar supports and compliments the teaching of our church as we seek to empower God's people to become fully devoted followers of Jesus Christ.

John Paulus
Director of Adult Education, Peace With Christ Lutheran
Church, Aurora, CO

Your seminar does a great job of educating people about the power of God's financial principles and the freedom they bring to life. Thanks so much for standing on His Word.

Jim Phillips
Senior Pastor, Mountainview Community Christian Church,
Highlands Ranch, CO

Many of the people in attendance have been talking about the information gained at the seminar and are very excited to begin "working their plans." I so appreciated your presentation of valuable financial information on debt reduction in addition to your approach towards good stewardship in the body of Christ.

Gary Jensen
Director of Family Life Ministries, Calvary Temple, Denver, CO

You helped my wife and me to get out of debt and into financial freedom.

Jeff Nelsen
Senior Pastor, Cherry Hills Baptist Church, Springfield, IL

We are on our way to being debt free, including our mortgage, in seven years. Additionally, our giving at the church has gone up exponentially since the workshop."

Kevin Navarro
Pastor, Bethany Evangelical Free Church,
Centennial, CO

About the Author

Bob Marette has been teaching God's Principles of Finance for over 20 years, and has counseled hundreds of couples and individuals drowning in debt. He has brought the life-changing workshop, "How to Get Out of Debt In Five to Seven Years, Including Mortgage" to hundreds of churches around the country. His daily one-minute radio program, "Out of Debt with Bob Marette" gives financial tips on how to get completely out of debt in just a few short years.

To view his current schedule, visit www.bobmarette.com. To schedule a workshop at your church anywhere in the United States or Canada, call 303-280-9565. Bob and his wife, Deborah, are proud parents and grandparents, and live in Denver, Colorado.

Photo by Kari Barrios

Back Cover Material

Three Steps to Becoming Debt Free in a Short Period of Time

There is a stress-free way to get totally out of debt in a short period of time. No dramatic life-style changes are necessary.

This is not a typical financial book; it is a debt-elimination book with a straightforward plan that will help every serious reader. You will learn:

- Common-sense wisdom
- How to avoid financial pitfalls and partner with God
- Two critical foundational principles
- Three simple steps to financial freedom

Marette's proven process will work. He shows you how to get completely out of debt in five to seven years, including mortgages, according to the principles outlined in God's Word.

Bob Marette is the President of Financial Health Fair, a non-pro t organization that is designed to "...bring the light of hope to the darkness of debt." He has taught the life-changing workshop, "How to Get Out of Debt in 5-7 Years, Including Mortgage" in over 300 churches, businesses, and colleges around the country. His book, *Scriptural Calendar: a Daily Guide to Help*

You Hide God's Word in Your Heart, is a tool that will help readers learn to memorize the Scriptures. You can hear Bob on his daily radio program, "Out of Debt With Bob Marette."

Made in United States
North Haven, CT
05 November 2026

21766940R00124